THE PHILANDERERS

A. E. W. MASON

1st WORLD
LIBRARY
Literary Society

The Philanderers

A. E. W. Mason

© 1st World Library, 2007
PO Box 2211
Fairfield, IA 52556
www.1stworldlibrary.com
First Edition

LCCN: 2007934076

Softcover ISBN: 978-1-4218-9605-2
Hardcover ISBN: 978-1-4218-9705-9
eBook ISBN: 978-1-4218-9505-5

Purchase *"The Philanderers"*
as a traditional bound book at:
www.1stWorldLibrary.com/purchase.asp?ISBN=978-1-4218-9605-2

1st World Library is a literary, educational organization
dedicated to:

- Creating a free internet library of downloadable ebooks

- Hosting writing competitions and offering book publishing
scholarships.

Interested in more 1st World Library books? contact:
literacy@1stworldlibrary.com
Check us out at: www.1stworldlibrary.com

1ˢᵗ World Library Literary Society

Giving Back to the World

"If you want to work on the core problem, it's early school literacy."

- James Barksdale, former CEO of Netscape

"No skill is more crucial to the future of a child, or to a democratic and prosperous society, than literacy."

- Los Angeles Times

"Literacy... means far more than learning how to read and write... The aim is to transmit... knowledge and promote social participation."

- UNESCO

"Literacy is not a luxury, it is a right and a responsibility. If our world is to meet the challenges of the twenty-first century we must harness the energy and creativity of all our citizens."

- President Bill Clinton

"Parents should be encouraged to read to their children, and teachers should be equipped with all available techniques for teaching literacy, so the varying needs and capacities of individual kids can be taken into account."

- Hugh Mackay

PROLOGUE

Five Englishmen were watching a camp fire in the centre of a forest clearing in mid-Africa. They did not speak, but sat propped against logs, smoking. One of the five knocked out the ashes of his pipe upon the ground; a second, roused by the movement, picked up a fresh billet of wood with a shiver and threw it on to the fire, and the light for a moment flung a steady glow upon faces which were set with anxiety. The man who had picked up the billet looked from one to the other of the faces, then he turned and gazed behind him into the darkness. The floor of the clearing was dotted with the embers of dying fires, but now and again he would hear the crackle of a branch and see a little flame spirt up and shine upon the barrels of rifles and the black bodies of the sleeping troops. Round the edge of the clearing the trees rose massed and dark like a cliff's face. He turned his head upwards.

'Look, Drake!' he cried suddenly, and pointed an arm eastwards. The man opposite to him took his pipe from his mouth and looked in that direction. The purple was fading out of the sky, leaving it livid.

'I see,' said Drake shortly, and, replacing his pipe, he rose to his feet. His four companions looked quickly at each other and the eldest of them spoke.

'Look here, Drake,' said he, 'I have been thinking about this business all night, and the more I think of it the less I like it. Of course, we only did what we were bound to do. We couldn't get behind that evidence; there was no choice for us; but you're the captain, and there is a choice for you.'

'No,' replied Drake quietly. 'I too have been thinking about it all night, and there is no choice for me.'

'But you can delay the execution until we get back.'

'I can't even do that. A week ago there was a village here.'

'It's not the man I am thinking of. I haven't lived my years in Africa to have any feeling left for scum like that. But also I haven't lived my years in Africa without coming to know there's one thing above all others necessary for the white man to do, and that's to keep up the prestige of the white man. String Gorley up if you like, but not here—not before these blacks.'

'But that's just what I am going to do,' answered Drake, 'and just for your reason, too—the prestige of the white man. Every day something is stolen by these fellows, a rifle, a bayonet, rations—something. When I find the theft out I have to punish it, haven't I? Well, how can I punish the black when he thieves, and let the white man off when he thieves and murders? If I did—well, I don't think I could strike a harder blow at the white man's prestige.'

'I don't ask you to let him off. Only take him back to the coast. Let him be hanged there privately.'

'And how many of these blacks would believe that he had been hanged?' Drake turned away from the group and walked towards a hut which stood some fifty yards from the camp

A. E. W. Mason

fire. Three sentries were guarding the door. Drake pushed the door open, entered, and closed it behind him. The hut was pitch dark since a board had been nailed across the only opening.

'Gorley!' he said.

There was a rustling of boughs against the opposite wall, and a voice answered from close to the ground.

'Damn you, what do you want?'

'Have you anything you wish to say?'

'That depends,' replied Gorley after a short pause, and his voice changed to an accent of cunning.

'There's no bargain to be made.'

The words were spoken with a sharp precision, and again there was a rustling of leaves as though Gorley had fallen back upon his bed of branches.

'But you can undo some of the harm,' continued Drake, and at that Gorley laughed. Drake stopped on the instant, and for a while there was silence between the pair. A gray beam of light shot through a chink between the logs, and then another and another until the darkness of the hut changed to a vaporous twilight. Then of a sudden the notes of a bugle sounded the reveille. Gorley raised himself upon his elbows and thrust forward his head. Outside he heard the rattle of arms, the chatter of voices, all the hum of a camp astir.

'Drake,' he whispered across to the figure standing against the door, 'there's enough gold dust to make two men rich, but you shall have it all if you let me go. You can—easily enough. It wouldn't be difficult for a man to slip away into the forest on the march back if you gave the nod to the sentries guarding him. All I ask for is a rifle and a belt of cartridges. I'd shift for myself then.'

He ended abruptly and crouched, listening to the orders shouted to the troops outside. The men were being ranged in their companies. Then the companies in succession were marched, halted, wheeled, and halted again. Gorley traced a plan of their evolutions with his fingers upon the floor of the hut. The companies were formed into a square.

'Drake,' he began again, and he crawled a little way across the hut; 'Drake, do you hear what I'm saying? There's a fortune for you, mind you, all of it; and I am the only one who can tell you where it is. I didn't trust those black fellows—no, no,' and he wagged his head with an attempt at an insinuating laugh. 'I had it all gathered together, and I buried it myself at night. You gave me a chance before with nothing to gain. Give me another; you have everything to gain this time. Drake, why don't you speak?'

'Because there's no bargain to be made between you and me,' replied Drake. 'If you tell me where the gold dust's hid, it will be given back to the people it belonged to, or rather to those of them you left alive. You can do some good that way by telling me, but you won't save your life.'

Steps were heard to approach the hut; there was a rap on the door.

'Well?' asked Drake.

Gorley raised himself from the floor.

'I am not making you rich and letting you kill me too,' he

A. E. W. Mason

said; and then, 'Who cares? I'm ready.'

Drake opened the door and stepped out. Gorley swaggered after him. He stood for a moment on the threshold. Here and there a wisp of fog ringed a tree-trunk or smoked upon the ground. But for the rest, the clearing, littered with the charred debris of a native village, lay bare and desolate in a cold morning light.

'It looks a bit untidy,' said Gorley, with a laugh. Two of the troopers approached and laid their hands upon his shoulders. At first he made a movement to shake them off. Then he checked the impulse and stood quietly while they pinioned him. After they had finished he spat on the ground, cast a glance at the square and the rope dangling from a branch above it, and walked easily towards it. The square opened to receive him and closed up again.

On the march back two of the Englishmen sickened of ague and died. Six months later a third was killed in a punitive expedition. The fourth was drowned off Walfisch Bay before another year had elapsed.

CHAPTER I

Hugh Fielding, while speculating upon certain obscure episodes in the history of a life otherwise familiar to an applauding public, and at a loss to understand them, caught eagerly at a simile. Now Fielding came second to none in his scorn for the simile as an explanation, possibly because he was so well acquainted with its convenience. 'A fairy lamp' he would describe it, quite conscious of the irony in his method of description, 'effective as an ornament upon a table-cloth, but a poor light to eat your dinner by.'

Nevertheless Fielding hugged this particular simile, applying it as a sort of skeleton key to the problem of Stephen Drake's career.

He compared Drake's career, or at all events that portion of it which was closed, to the writing of a book. So many years represent the accumulation of material, a deliberate accumulation; at a certain date the book is begun with a settled design, *finis* being clearly foreseen from the first word of the preface. But once fairly started the book throws the writer on one side and takes the lead, drags him, panting and protesting, after it, flings him down by-ways out of sight of his main road, tumbles him into people he had no thought of meeting, and finally stops him dead, Heaven knows where—in front of a blank wall, most likely, at the end of a

A. E. W. Mason

cul de sac. He may sit down then and cry if he likes, but to that point he has come in spite of his intentions.

The actual settling down to the work, with the material duly ticketed at his elbow, in Drake's case Hugh Fielding dated back to a certain day towards the close of October.

Upon that afternoon the *Dunrobin Castle* from Cape Town steamed into Plymouth Harbour, and amongst the passengers one man stepped from the tender on to the quay and stood there absolutely alone. No one had gone out to the ship to meet him; no one came forward now on the quay-side, and it was evident from his indifference to the bystanders that he expected no one. The more careless of these would have accounted him a complete stranger to the locality, the more observant an absentee who had just returned, for while his looks expressed isolation, one significant gesture proved familiarity with the environments. As his eyes travelled up the tiers of houses and glanced along towards the Hoe, they paused now and again and rested upon any prominent object as though upon a remembered landmark, and each such recognition he emphasised with a nod of the head.

He turned his back towards the town, directing his glance in a circle. The afternoon, although toning to dusk, was kept bright by the scouring of a keen wind, and he noted the guard-ship on his right at its old moorings, the funnels rising like solid yellow columns from within a stockade of masts; thence he looked across the water to the yellowing woods of Mount Edgcumbe, watched for a moment or so the brown sails of the fishing-smacks dancing a *chassez-croisez* in the Sound, and turned back to face the hill-side. A fellow-passenger, hustled past him by half a dozen importunate children, extricated a hand to wave, and shouted a cheery 'See you in town, Drake.' Drake roused himself with a start and took a step in the same direction; he was confronted by a man in a Norfolk jacket and tweed knickerbockers, who, standing by, had caught the name.

'Captain Stephen Drake?'

'Yes. Why?'

The man mopped a perspiring face.

'I was afraid I had missed you. I should have gone out on the tender, only I was late. Can you spare me a moment? You have time.'

'Certainly,' answered Drake, with a look of inquiry.

The man in the knickerbockers led the way along the quay until he came to an angle between an unused derrick and a wall.

'We shall not be disturbed here,' he said, and he drew an oblong note-book and a cedar-wood pencil from his pocket.

'I begin to understand,' said Drake, with a laugh.

'You can have no objection?'

There was the suavity of the dentist who holds the forceps behind his back in the tone of the speaker's voice.

'On the contrary, a little notoriety will be helpful to me too.'

That word 'too' jarred on the reporter, suggesting a flippancy which he felt to be entirely out of place. The feeling, however, was quickly swallowed up in the satisfaction which he experienced at obtaining so easily a result which had threatened the need of diplomacy.

A. E. W. Mason

'*O si sic omnes!*' he exclaimed, and made a note of the quotation upon the top of the open leaf.

'Surely the quotation is rather hackneyed to begin with?' suggested Drake with a perfectly serious inquisitiveness. The reporter looked at him suspiciously.

'We have to consider our readers,' he replied with some asperity.

'By the way, what paper do you represent?'

The reporter hesitated a little.

'The *Evening Meteor*,' he admitted reluctantly, keeping a watchful eye upon his questioner. He saw the lips join in a hard line, and began to wonder whether, after all, the need for diplomacy had passed.

'I begin to appreciate the meaning of journalistic enterprise,' said Drake. 'Your editor makes a violent attack upon me, and then sends a member of his staff to interview me the moment I set foot in England.'

'You hardly take the correct view, if I may say so. Our chief when he made the attacks acted under a sense of responsibility, and he thought it only fair that you should have the earliest possible opportunity of making your defence.'

'I beg your pardon,' replied Drake gravely. 'Your chief is the most considerate of men, and I trust that his equity will leave him a margin of profit, only I don't seem to feel that I need make any defence. I have no objection to be interviewed, as I told you, but you must make it clear that I intend nothing in the way of apology. Is that understood?'

The pressman agreed, and made a note of the proviso.

'There is another point. I have seen nothing of the paper necessarily for the last few weeks. The *Meteor* has, I suppose, continued its—crusade, shall we call it?—but on what lines exactly I am, of course, ignorant. It will be better, consequently, that you should put questions and I answer them, upon this condition, however,—that all reference is omitted to any point on which I am unwilling to speak.'

The reporter demurred, but, seeing that Drake was obdurate, he was compelled to give way.

'The entire responsibility of the expedition rests with me,' Drake explained, 'but there were others concerned in it. You might trench upon private matters which only affect them.'

He watched the questions with the vigilance of a counsel on behalf of a client undergoing cross-examination, but they were directed solely to the elucidation of the disputed point whether Drake had or had not, while a captain in the service of the Matanga Republic, attacked a settlement of Arab slave-dealers within the zone of a British Protectorate. The editor of the *Meteor* believed that he had, and strenuously believed it—in the interests of his shareholders. Drake, on the other hand, and the Colonial Office, it should be added, were dispassionately indifferent to the question, for the very precise reason that they knew it could never be decided. There were doubts as to the exact sphere of British influence, and the doubts favoured Drake for the most part. Insular prehensiveness, at its highest flight, could do no more than claim Boruwimi as its uttermost limit, and was aware it would be hard put to it to substantiate the claim. The editor, nevertheless, persevered, bombarded its citizen readers with warnings about trade fleeing from lethargic empires, published a cartoon, and reluctantly took the blackest view of Drake's character and aims.

Drake's march with a handful of men six hundred miles through a tangled forest had been a handsome exploit, quickening British pride with the spectacle of an Englishman at the head of it. Civilian blood tingled in office and shop, claiming affinity with Drake's. It needed an Englishman to bill-hook a path through that fretwork of branches, and fall upon his enemy six weeks before he was expected—the true combination of daring and endurance that stamps the race current coin across the world! Economy also pleaded for Drake. But for him the country itself must have burned out the hornets' nest, and the tax-payer paid, and paid dearly. For there would have been talk of the expedition beforehand, the force would have found an enemy prepared and fortified. The hornets could sting too! Whereas Drake had burned them out before they had time to buzz. He need not have said one word in exculpation of himself, and that indeed he knew. But he had interests and ambitions of his own to serve; a hint of them peeped out.

'As to your future plans?' asked the reporter. 'You mean to go back, I presume.'

'No; London for me, if I can find a corner in it. I hold concessions in Matanga.'

'The land needs development, of course.'

'Machinery too; capital most of all.'

At the bookstall upon the platform Drake bought a copy of the *Times*, and whilst taking his change he was attracted by a grayish-green volume prominently displayed upon the white newspapers. The sobriety of the binding caught his fancy. He picked it up, and read the gold-lettered title on the back—*A*

Man of Influence. The stall-keeper recommended the novel; he had read it himself; besides, it was having a sale. Drake turned to the title-page and glanced at the author's name— Sidney Mallinson. He flashed into enthusiasm.

'Selling, eh?'

'Very well indeed.'

'Has it been published long?'

'Less than three months.'

'I will take it, and everything else by the same author.'

'It is his first book.'

The stall-keeper glanced at his enthusiastic customer, and saw a sunburnt face, eager as a boy's.

'Oh!' he said doubtfully, 'I don't know whether you will like it. It's violently modern. Perhaps this,' and he suggested with an outstretched forefinger a crimson volume explained by its ornamentation of a couple of assegais bound together with a necklace of teeth. Drake laughed at the application of the homoeopathic principle to the sale of books.

'No, I will take this,' he said, and, moving aside from the stall, stood for a little turning the book over and over in his hands, feeling its weight and looking incessantly at the title-page, wondering, you would say, that the author had accomplished so much.

He had grounds for wonder, too. His thoughts went back across the last ten years, and he remembered Mallinson's clamouring for a reputation; a name—that had been the essential thing, no matter what the career in which it was to be won. Work he had classified according to the opportunities it afforded of public recognition; and his classification varied from day to day. A *cause celebre* would suggest the Bar, a published sermon the Church, a flaming poster persuade to the stage. In a word, he had looked upon a profession as no more than a sounding-board.

It had always seemed to Drake that this fervid desire for fame, as a thing apart in itself, not as a symbol of success won in a cherished pursuit, argued some quality of weakness in the man, something unstable which would make for failure. His surprise was increased by an inability to recollect that Mallinson had ever considered literature as a means to his end. Long sojourning in the wilderness, moreover, had given Drake an exaggerated reverence for the printed page. He was inclined to set Mallinson on a pinnacle, and scourge himself at the foot of it for his earlier distrust of him. He opened the book again at the beginning, and let the pages slip across beneath his thumb from cover to cover; 413 was marked on the top corner of the last; 413 pages actually written and printed and published; all consecutive too; something new on each page. He turned to a porter.

'How long have I before the train starts?'

'Five minutes, sir.'

'Where is the telegraph office?'

The office was pointed out to him, and he telegraphed to Mallinson at the address of his publishers. 'Have just reached England. Dine with me at eight to-morrow at the Grand Hotel'; and he added after a moment's pause, 'Bring Conway, if you have not lost sight of him.—DRAKE.'

When the train started Drake settled himself to the study of *A Man of Influence*. The commentary of the salesman had prepared him for some measure of perplexity. There would be hinted references and suggestions, difficult of comprehension to the traveller out of touch with modern developments. These, however, would only be the ornaments, but the flesh and blood of the story would be perceptible enough. It was just, however, this very flesh and blood which eluded him; he could not fix it in a definite form. He did not hold the key to the author's intention.

Drake's *vis-a-vis* in the carriage saw him produce the book with considerable surprise, conscious of an incongruity between the reader and what he read. His surprise changed to amusement as he noticed Drake's face betray his perplexity and observed him turn now and again to the title upon the cover as though doubtful whether he had not misread it. He gave an audible chuckle.

Drake looked up and across the carriage at a man of about fifty years of age with a large red face and a close-cropped pointed beard. The chuckle swelled to a laugh.

'You find that a hard nut to crack?' Drake noticed a thickness in the articulation.

'I have been some years abroad. I hardly catch its drift,' explained Drake, and then with an effort at praise:

'It seems a clever satire.'

'Satire!' guffawed the other. 'Well, that's rich! Satire? Why, it's a manifesto. Gad, sir, it's a creed. I believe in my duty to my senses and the effectuation of me for ever and ever, Amen. The modern jargon! Topsy Turvydom! Run the world on the comic opera principle, but be flaming serious about it.

A. E. W. Mason

Satire, good Lord!'

He flung himself back on his cushions with a snort of contempt.

'Look you, I'm not a pess—' he checked at the word and then took it at a run, 'a pessimist, but, as things are going on—well, you have been out of the country and—and you can't help it, I suppose. You may laugh! P'raps you haven't got daughters—not that I have either, praise glory! But nieces, if the father's a fool, wear you out very little less. Satire, ho! ho!'

The semi-intoxicated uncle of nieces relapsed vindictively into his corner and closed his eyes. Occasionally Drake would hear a muffled growl, and, looking in that direction, would see one inflamed eye peering from a mountain of rugs.

'Satire!' and a husky voice would address the passengers indiscriminately. 'Satire! and the man's not a day under forty either.'

Drake joined in the laugh and lit his pipe. He was not sensitive to miscomputations of his years, and felt disinclined to provoke further outbursts of family confidences.

Instead, he pursued his acquaintance with *A Man of Influence*, realising now that he must take him seriously and regard him stamped with Mallinson's approval, a dominating being. He found the task difficult. The character insisted upon reminding him of the nursery-maid's ideal, the dandified breaker of hearts and bender of wills; an analytical hero too, who traced the sentence through the thought to the emotion, which originally prompted it; whence his success and influence. But for his strength, plainly aimed at by the author, and to be conceded by the reader, if the book was to convince? Drake compared him to scree and shingle as against solid granite. Lean on him and you slip!

The plot was the time-worn, imperishable story of the married couple and the amorous interloper, the Influential Man, of course, figuring as the latter, and consequently glorified. The husband was pelted with ridicule from the first chapter to the last, though for what particular fault Drake could not discover, unless it were for that of being a husband at all; so that the interloper in robbing him of his wife was related to have secured not merely the *succes d'estime* which accompanies such enviable feats, but the unqualified gratitude of all married women and most unmarried men.

There were, no doubt, redeeming qualities; Drake gave them full credit, and perhaps more than they deserved. He noticed a glitter in the dialogue, whether of foil or gold he refused to consider, and a lively imagination in the interweaving of the incidents. But altogether the book left with him a feeling of distaste, which was not allayed by the perception that he himself was caricatured in the picture of befooled husband, while Mallinson figured as the successful deceiver. After all, he thought, Mallinson and he were friends, and he disliked the mere imagining of such a relationship between them.

Drake summed up his impressions as his hansom turned into the Bayswater Road. The day was just beginning to break; the stems of the trees bordering the park were black bars against the pure, colourless light, and their mingling foliage a frayed black ribbon stretched across the sky. One might have conceived the picture the original of a black and white drawing by a pre-Raphaelite artist.

Drake drew in a long breath of the keen, clear air.

'I am glad I asked him to bring Conway,' he said to himself.

CHAPTER II

Waking up six hours later, Drake looked out upon a brown curtain of London fog. The lamps were lit at the crossings in Trafalgar Square—half-a-mile distant they seemed, opaque haloes about a pin's point of flame, and people passing in the light of them loomed and vanished like the figures of a galanty-show. From beneath rose the bustle of the streets, perceptible only to Drake, upon the fourth floor, as a subterranean rumble. 'London,' he said to himself, 'I live here,' and laughed unappalled. Listening to the clamour, he remembered a map, seen somewhere in a railway guide, a map of England with the foreign cables, tiny spider-threads spun to the four quarters and thickening to a solid column at Falmouth and Cromer, the world's arteries, he liked to think, converging to its heart.

The notion of messages flashing hourly along these wires brought to mind the existence of the *Meteor*. He sent out for a copy of each number which had appeared since he had begun his voyage, and commencing on the task whilst he was still at breakfast, read through every article written concerning the Boruwimi expedition. He finished the last in the smoking-room shortly after one o'clock, and rose from his investigation with every appearance of relief. From the first to the final paragraph, not so much as a mention of Gorley's name!

The reason for his relief lay in a promise which he had sent to Gorley's father, that he would suppress the trouble as far as he could; and Drake liked to keep his promises.

Gorley had come out to Matanga with a cloudy reputation winging close at his heels. There were rumours of dishonesty in the office of a private bank in Kent; his name became a sign for silence, and you were allowed to infer that Gorley's relatives had made good the deficit and so avoided a criminal prosecution. It was not surprising, then, that Gorley, on hearing of Drake's intended march to Boruwimi, should wish to take service under his command. He called upon Drake with that request, was confronted with the current story, and invited to disprove it. Gorley read his man shrewdly, and confessed the truth of the charge without an attempt at mitigation. He asked frankly for a place in the troop, the lowest, as his chance of redemption, or rather demanded it as a grace due from man to man. Drake was taken by his manner, noticed his build, which was tough and wiry, and conceded the request. Nor had he reason to regret his decision on the march out. Gorley showed himself alert, and vigilant, a favourite with the blacks, and obedient to his officers. He was advanced from duty to duty; a week before the force began its homeward march from Boruwimi he was sent out with a body of men to forage for provisions. Three days later a solitary negro rushed into camp, one of the few survivors of his tribe, he said. He told a story of food freely given, a village plundered and burned for thanks, of gold-dust stolen and the owners murdered that they might the better hold their tongues. He signified Gorley as the culprit. Drake, guided by the negro, marched towards the spot. He met Gorley and his company half-way between Boruwimi and the village, carried him along with him, and proved the story true. Against Gorley's troops no charge could be sustained; they had only obeyed orders. But Gorley he court-martialled, and the result has been described.

A. E. W. Mason

This was the incident which Drake was unwilling to commit to the discretion of the editor of the *Meteor*. He had discovered Gorley's relations in England, and had written to them a full account of the affair, despatching with his letter a copy of the evidence given at the court-martial. The reply came from the father, a heart-broken admission of the justice of Drake's action, and a prayer that, for the sake of those of the family who still lived, Gorley's crime should be as far as possible kept secret. Drake gave the promise. So far he had kept it, he realised, as he tossed aside the last copy of the *Meteor*.

At eight o'clock Sidney Mallinson arrived. He saw Drake at the top of the flight of steps in the vestibule, and hesitated, perceiving that he was alone.

'Hasn't Conway come?' he asked. 'I sent to him.'

'Not yet. It's barely eight.'

They shook hands limply and searched for topics of conversation.

'You look older than you did,' said Mallinson.

'Ah! Ten years, you know. You haven't changed much.'

Drake was looking at a face distinguished by considerable comeliness. The forehead, however, overhung the features beneath it and gave to a mouth and chin, which would otherwise have aroused no criticism, an appearance of irresolution. The one noticeable difference in Mallinson was the addition of an air of constraint. It was due partly to a question which had troubled him since he had received the invitation. Had Drake read *A Man of Influence* and recognised himself?

'I got your telegram,' he said at length.

'Naturally, or you wouldn't be here.'

The answer was intended to be jocular; it sounded only *gauche*, as Drake recognised, and the laugh which accompanied it positively rude.

'Shall I put my coat in the cloak-room?' suggested Mallinson.

'Oh yes, do!' replied Drake. He was inclined to look upon the proposal as an inspiration, and his tone unfortunately betrayed his thought.

When Mallinson returned, he saw Conway entering the hotel. The latter looked younger by some years than either of his companions, so that, as the three men stood together at this moment, they might have been held to represent three separate decades.

'Twenty minutes late, I'm afraid,' said Conway, and he shook Drake's hand with a genuine cordiality.

'Five,' said Drake, looking at his watch.

'Twenty,' replied Conway. 'A quarter to, was the time Mallinson wired me.'

'Was it?' asked Mallinson, with a show of surprise. 'I must have made a mistake.'

It occurred, however, to Drake that the mistake might have been purposely made from a prevision of the awkwardness of the meeting. The dinner, prefaced inauspiciously, failed to remove the awkwardness, since the reticence under which Drake and Mallinson laboured, gradually spread and enveloped Conway. A forced conversation of a curiously impersonal sort dragged from course to course. Absolute strangers would have exhibited less restraint; for the ghost of an old comradeship made the fourth at the feast and prated to them in exiguous voice of paths that had diverged. Drake noticed, besides, an undercurrent of antagonism between Conway and Mallinson. He inquired what each had been doing during his absence.

'Mallinson,' interposed Conway, 'has been absorbed in the interesting study of his own personality.'

'I am not certain that pursuit is not preferable to revolving unsuccessfully through a cycle of professions,' said Mallinson in slow sarcasm.

The flush was upon Conway's cheek now. He set his wine glass deliberately upon the table and leaned forward on an elbow.

'My dear good Sidney,' he began with elaborate affection, plainly intended as the sugar coating of an excessively unpleasant pill. Drake hastily interrupted with an anecdote of African experiences. It sounded bald and monstrously long, but it served its purpose as peace-maker. Literary acquisitiveness drew Mallinson on to ask for more of the same kind. Drake mentioned a race of pigmies and described them, speculating whether they might be considered the originals of the human race.

'My dear fellow, don't!' said Mallinson; 'I loathe hearing about them. It's so degrading to us to think we sprang from them.'

The peculiar sensitiveness of a mind ever searching, burrowing in, and feeding upon itself struck a jarring note upon its healthier companion.

'Why, what on earth does it matter?' asked Drake.

'Ah! Perhaps you wouldn't understand.'

Conway gave a shrug of the shoulder and laughed to Drake across the table. The latter looked entreaty in reply and courageously started a different topic. He spoke of their boyhood in the suburb on the heights six miles to the south of London, and in particular of a certain hill, Elm-tree Hill they called it, a favourite goal for walks and the spot where the three had last met on the night before Drake left England. London had lain beneath it roped with lights.

'The enchanted city,' said Conway, catching back some flavour of those times. 'It seemed distant as El Dorado, and as desirable.'

Mallinson responded with the gentle smile with which a man recognises and pities a childishness he has himself outgrown.

Drake ordered port, having great faith in its qualities, as inducive of a cat-like content and consequent good-fellowship. Mallinson, however, never touched port; nothing but the lightest of French burgundies after dinner for him. The party withdrew to the smoking-room.

'By the way, Drake,' asked Mallinson, 'have you anything to do to-night?'

'No, why?'

'I was asked to take you to a sort of party.'

Conway looked up sharply in surprise.

'You were asked to take me!' exclaimed Drake. 'Who asked you?'

'Oh, nobody whom you know.' He hesitated for a second, then added with studied carelessness, 'A Miss Le Mesurier. Her mother's dead,' he explained, noticing the look of surprise on Drake's face, 'so she keeps house for her father. There's an aunt to act as chaperon, but she doesn't count. I got a note from Miss Le Mesurier just before I came here asking me to bring you.'

'But what does she know of me?'

'Oh, I may have mentioned your name,' he explained indifferently, and Conway smiled.

'Besides,' said Conway, 'the *Meteor* has transformed you into a public character. One knows of your movements.'

'What I don't see is how Miss Le Mesurier could have known that you had landed yesterday,' commented Mallinson.

'I was interviewed by the *Meteor* on Plymouth Quay. You received the note, you say, this evening. She may have seen the interview.'

Drake called to a waiter and ordered him to bring a copy of the paper. Conway took it and glanced at the first page.

'Yes, here it is.'

He read a few lines to himself, and burst into a laugh.

'Guess how it begins?'

'I know,' said Drake.

'A sovereign you don't.'

Drake laid a sovereign on the table. Conway followed his example.

'It begins,' said Drake, 'with a Latin quotation, *O si sic omnes*!'

'It begins,' corrected Conway, pocketing the money, 'with very downright English'; and he read, 'Drake, with the casual indifference of the hardened filibuster, readily accorded an interview to our representative on landing from the *Dunrobin Castle* yesterday afternoon!'

Drake snatched the paper out of Conway's hand, and ran his eye down the column to see whether his words had been similarly transmuted by the editorial alchemy. They were printed, however, as they had been spoken, but interspersed with comments. The editor had contented himself with stamping his own device upon the coin; he had not tried to change its metal. Drake tossed the paper on one side. 'The man goes vitriol-throwing with vinegar,' he said.

Conway picked up the *Meteor*.

'You are a captain, aren't you?' he asked. 'The omission of the title presumes you a criminal.'

'I don't object to the omission,' replied Drake. 'I suppose the title belongs to me by right. But, after all, a captain in Matanga! There are more honourable titles.'

Mallinson looked at him suddenly, as though some fresh idea had shot into his brain.

'Well, will you come?' he asked carelessly.

'I hardly feel inclined to move.'

'I didn't imagine you would.' There was evidence of distinct relief in the brisk tone of Mallinson's voice. He turned to Conway, 'We ought to be starting, I fancy.'

'I shall stay with Drake,' Conway answered, despondently to Drake's thinking, and he lapsed into silence after Mallinson's departure, broken by intervals of ineffective sarcasm concerning women, ineffectively accentuated by short jerks of laughter. He roused himself in a while and carried Drake off to his club, where he found Hugh Fielding pulling his moustache over the *Meteor*. He introduced Drake, and left them together.

'I was reading a list of your sins,' said Fielding, and he waved the newspaper.

Drake laughed in reply.

'The vivisectionists,' said Fielding, 'may cite you as proof of the painlessness of their work.'

'It is my character that suffers the knife. I fancy the editor would prefer to call the operation a *post-mortem*.'

Fielding warmed to his new acquaintance. Whisky and potass helped them to discover common friends, about whom Fielding supplied information with a flavour of acid in his talk which commended him to Drake; it bit without malice. Mallinson's name was mentioned.

'You have read his autobiography?' asked Fielding.

'No; but I have read his novel.'

'That's what I mean. Most men wait till they have achieved a career before they write their autobiographies. He anticipates his. It's rather characteristic of the man, I think.'

They drove from the club together in a hansom. Opposite to his rooms in St. James's Street Fielding got out.

'Good-night,' he said, and took a step towards the door.

A lukewarm curiosity which had been stirring in Drake during the latter part of the evening prompted him to a question now that he saw the opportunity to satisfy it disappearing.

'You know the Le Mesuriers?' he asked.

Fielding laughed. 'Already?' he said.

'I don't understand.'

'Then you are not acquainted with the lady?'

'No; that's what I'm asking. What is Miss Le Mesurier like?'

'She is more delightfully surprising than even I had imagined. Otherwise she's difficult to describe; a bald enumeration of features would be rank injustice.'

Drake's curiosity responded to the flick.

'One might fit them together with a little trouble,' he suggested.

'The metaphor of a puzzle is not inapt,' replied Fielding, as he opened his door. 'Good-night!' and he went in.

A. E. W. Mason

Half-way down Pall Mall Drake was smitten by a sudden impulse. The fog had cleared from the streets; he looked up at the sky. The night was moonless but starlit, and very clear. He lifted the trap, spoke to the cabman, and in a few minutes was driving southwards across Westminster Bridge.

It was the chance recollection of a phrase dropped by Conway during dinner which sent him in this untimely scurry to Elm-tree Hill. 'As distant as El Dorado, and as desirable.' The sentence limned with precision the impression which London used to produce upon Drake. The sight of it touched upon some single chord of fancy in a nature otherwise prosaic, of which the existence was unsuspected by his few companions and unrealised by himself.

Working in that tower which you could see from the summit of the Elm-tree Hill topping the sky-line to the west, in order to complete his education as an engineer before his meagre capital was exhausted, Drake had enjoyed little opportunity of acquiring knowledge of London; and those acquaintances of his who travelled thither with their shiny black bags every morning, seemed to him to know even less than he did. There were but two points of view from which the town was regarded in the suburb, and the inhabitants chose this view according to their sex. To the men London was a counting-house, and certainly some miles of yellow brick mansions and flashing glasshouses testified that the view was a profitable one. To the women it was the alluringly wicked abode of society, and they held their hands before their faces when they mentioned it, to hide their yearning. Occasionally they imagined they caught a glimpse into it, when a minister from one of the states in the Balkan Peninsula strayed down to shed a tallow-candle lustre over a garden party. To both these views Drake had listened with the air of a man listening to an impertinence, and his attitude towards the former view showed particularly the strength of the peculiar impression which London made on him, since he always placed the acquisition of a fortune as an aim before himself.

He thought of London, in fact, as a countryman might, with all a countryman's sense of its mystery and romance, intensified in him by the daily sight of its domes and spires. He saw it clothed by the changing seasons, now ringed in green, now shrouded in white; on summer mornings, when it lay clearly defined like a finished model and the sun sparkled on the vanes, set the long lines of windows ablaze in the Houses of Parliament, and turned the river into a riband of polished steel; or, again, when the cupola of St. Paul's and the Clock Tower at Westminster pierced upwards through a level of fog, as though hung in the mid-air; or when mists, shredded by a south wind, swirled and writhed about the rooftops until the city itself seemed to take fantastic shapes and melt to a substance no more solid than the mists themselves.

These pictures, deeply impressed upon him at the moment of actual vision, remained with Drake during the whole period of his absence, changing a little, no doubt, as his imagination more and more informed them, but losing nothing of vividness, rather indeed waxing in it with the gradual years. One may think of him as he marched on expeditions against hostile tribes, dwelling upon these recollections as upon the portrait of an inherited homestead. London, in fact, became to him a living motive, a determining factor in any choice of action. Whatsoever ambitions he nourished presumed London as their starting-point. It was then after all not very singular that on this first night of his return he should make a pilgrimage to the spot whence he had drawn such vital impressions. For a long time he stood looking down the grass slope ragged with brambles and stunted trees, and comprehending the whole lighted city in his glance.

A. E. W. Mason

On the way home his mind, which soon tired of a plunge into sentiment, reverted to the thought of Miss Le Mesurier, and he speculated unsuccessfully on the motive which had prompted her to send him so immediate an invitation. The enigmatic interest which she took in him, gave to him in fact a very definite interest in her. He wondered again what she was like. Fielding's description helped to pique his curiosity. All that he knew of her was her surname, and he found it impossible to infer a face or even a figure from this grain of knowledge. By the time he reached the Grand Hotel, he was regretting that he had not accepted her invitation.

CHAPTER III

Drake repeated his question to Fielding two days later, after a dinner with Conway at his club, but in a tone of languid interest.

'Why don't you ask Mallinson?' said Fielding. 'He knows her better than I do.'

Conway contested the assertion with some heat.

'Besides,' added Drake, 'his imagination may have been at work. About women, I prefer the estimate of a man of the world.'

The phrase was distasteful to a gentleman whose ambition it was to live and to be recognised as living within view of, but outside the world, say just above it in a placid atmosphere of his own creation. Fielding leaned back in his chair to mete out punishment, joining the finger-tips with an air of ordering a detailed statement.

'The inhabitants of Sark,' he began, 'were from immemorial times notable not merely for their predatory instincts, but for the stay-at-home fashion in which they gave those instincts play. They did not scour the seas for their victims, neither did they till their island. There was no need for so much exertion. They lay supine upon their rocks and waited until a sail appeared above the horizon. Even then they did not stir till nightfall. But after it was dark, they lighted bonfires upon suitable promontories, especially towards Brecqhou and the Gouliot channel, where snags are numerous, and gathered in their harvest in the morning.

'But,' Drake interrupted, 'what on earth has that to do with—'

'Miss Le Mesurier? A great deal, as you will see if you listen patiently. Lloyd's at that time had not been invented, and the Sarkese were consequently unpopular with the trading community, and in the reign of Henry the—well, the particular Henry is immaterial—an irate band of merchants sailed from Winchelsea on a trip. They depopulated Sark in a single night, as they thought. But they were mistaken. One family escaped their attention,—the Le Mesuriers, who were the custodians of the silver mines—' At this point Conway broke in with an impatient laugh. Fielding turned a quiet eye upon him and repeated in an even voice, 'Who were the custodians of the silver mines, and lived under the shelter of a little cliff close by the main shaft. When Helier de Carteret, who, you know,' and he inclined suavely towards Conway, 'was Seigneur of somewhere or other in Jersey, came a few years later to colonise Sark, he found the Le Mesuriers in possession, and while he confiscated the mines, he allowed them to retain their ancient dignity of custodians.'

'Fudge!' said Conway rudely. Fielding waved a deprecating hand and continued:

'Living where they did, it is not to be wondered at that the Le Mesuriers became gradually rich, and the De Carterets gradually poor, so that when the latter family was compelled to place the Seigneurie of Sark upon the market, the Le Mesuriers were the highest bidders. The Le Mesuriers thus became Seigneurs of Sark. But with their position they reversed their conduct, and, instead of taking other people's money out of mines, they put their own in, with the result that they sustained embarrassing losses. I mention these details incidentally to show that Miss Le Mesurier of to-day is directly descended from ancestors of predatory instincts, who did not go a-hunting for victims, but unobtrusively attracted them in a passive, lazy way which was none the less effectual.'

Conway's patience was exhausted at this period of the disquisition.

'I never heard such a hotch-potch of nonsense in my life,' he said.

'I admit,' returned Fielding with unruffled complacency, 'that I aimed at an allegory rather than a pedantic narrative of facts. I was endeavouring to explain Clarice Le Mesurier on the fashionable principle of heredity.'

It flashed across Drake that if Fielding had described, though with some exaggeration, an actual phase of Miss Le Mesurier's character, she must have been driven to make the first advance towards his acquaintance by a motive of unusual urgency. The notion, however, did but flash and flicker out. He had no mental picture of the girl to fix her within his view; he knew not, in fact, whether she was girl or woman. She was to him just an abstraction, and Drake was seldom inclined for the study of abstractions. His curiosity might, perhaps, have been stronger had Mallinson related to him the way in which he had been received at the house of the Le Mesuriers after his dinner with Drake. When he arrived he found the guests staring hard at each other silently, with the vacant expression which comes of an effort to understand a recitation in a homely dialect from the north of the Tweed. He waited in the doorway and suddenly saw Miss Le Mesurier rise from an embrasure in the window and take half a step towards him. Then she paused and resumed her seat.

'That's because I come alone,' he thought, and something more than his vanity was hurt.

The recitation reached its climax. Darby and Joan, quarrelling through nineteen stanzas as to whether they had been disturbed by a rat or a mouse, discovered in the twentieth that the animal was a ball of wool. The company sighed their relief in a murmur of thanks, and Mallinson crossed the room to the window.

'And Captain Drake?' Clarice asked as she gave him her hand. The disappointment in her voice irritated him, and he answered with a sharp petulance.

'He's not a captain really, you know.'

The girl glanced at him in surprise.

'I mean,' he went on, answering the glance, 'Of course he held the rank over there. But a captain in Matanga!' He shrugged his shoulders. 'There are more honourable titles.'

'Still I asked you to bring him. You got my note, I suppose?' Her manner signified a cold request for an explanation.

'I couldn't,' he replied shortly.

'You mean you did not think it worth while to take enough trouble to find him.'

'No; that's not the reason. In fact I dined with him to-night, but I saw that I couldn't bring him here.'

'Why?'

'Well, he's changed.'

'In what way?'

'He has grown so hopelessly bourgeois.'

The epithet was a light to Clarice. She knew it for the superlative in Mallinson's grammar of abuse. Bourgeois! The term was the palm of a hand squashed upon a lighted candle; it snuffed you out. Convicted of bourgeoisie, you ought to tinkle a bell for the rest of your life, or at the easiest be confined east of Temple Bar. Applied to Drake the word connoted animosity pure and simple, animosity suddenly conceived too, for it was not a week since Mallinson had been boasting of his friendship with the man. What was the reason of that animosity? Clarice lowered her eyelashes demurely and smiled.

'I fancied he was your friend,' she said with inquiring innocence.

'I believe I remarked that he was changed.' Mallinson looked up at a corner of the ceiling as he spoke, and the exasperation was more than ever pronounced in his voice.

'Mr. Drake,' she went on, and she laid the slightest possible emphasis on the prefix, 'Mr. Drake has travelled among the natives a good deal, I think you told me?'

'Yes.'

'It's funny that that should make a man bourgeois.'

Mallinson became flippant.

'I am not so sure,' he said. 'The natives, I should think, are essentially bourgeois. They love beads, and that's typical of the class. Evil communications, you know,' and he laughed, but awkwardly and without merriment.

'Really?' asked Clarice, looking straight at him with grave eyes. She seemed to be seriously deliberating the truth of his remark. Mallinson's laughter stopped short. 'There's my aunt beckoning to you,' she said.

Later in the evening she relented towards him, salving her disappointment with the flattery of his jealousy. She did not, however, relinquish on that account her intention to make Stephen Drake's acquaintance. She merely postponed it, trusting that the tides of accident would drift them together, as indeed they did, though after a longer delay than she had anticipated.

The occasion of their meeting was provided by the visit of a French actress to one of the London theatres. Drake and Conway edged into their stalls just before the curtain rose on a performance of *Frou-Frou*. During the first act the theatre gradually filled, and when the lights were turned up at its close only one box was empty. It was upon the first tier next to the stage. A few minutes after the second act had begun Conway nudged Drake and nodded towards the box.

'You asked what Miss Le Mesurier was like. There's your answer.'

Drake glanced in that direction. He saw a girl in a dress of pink silk, standing in the front of the box, with her hands upon the ledge and leaning her head a little forwards beyond it. The glare striking up from the stage beneath her gave a burnish of copper to her hair and a warm light to her face. She seemed of a fragile figure and with features regular and delicate. Drake received a notion of unimpressive prettiness and turned his attention to the stage. When the lights were raised again in the auditorium, he noticed that Fielding was in the box talking to a gentleman with white hair, and that Mallinson was seated by the side of Miss Le Mesurier. The latter couple were gazing about the house and apparently discussing the audience,—at all events conversing with considerable animation. Drake commented upon their manner and drew the conventional inference.

'Oh dear, no!' answered Conway energetically. 'Of course Mallinson's aim is apparent enough, poor fellow.' A touch of scorn in the voice, which rang false, negatived the pity of the phrase. 'But I don't suppose for an instant that she has realised it. She would be the last to do so. No, she has a fad in her head about authors just for the moment.'

'Oh!' said Drake, turning with some interest to his companion. 'Does that account for *A Man of Influence*?'

'Yes,' replied Conway reluctantly, 'I fancy it does.'

'I wondered what set him to writing.'

'He was at the Bar when he met her. I believe she persuaded him to write the book and give up the Law.'

'She is undertaking a pretty heavy responsibility.'

Conway looked at his friend and laughed.

'I'm afraid you won't find that she takes that view, nor indeed do I see why she should. Mallinson was doing no good— well, not much anyway—at the Bar. He has scored by following her advice. So if she ever had any responsibility, which I don't admit, for there was no compulsion on him to obey, his luck has already wiped it out.'

'I suppose the white-haired man's her father,' said Drake.

'Yes. There's another sister, but she's at school in Brussels.'

'How did you come across them?'

'Mallinson and I met them one summer when we were taking a holiday at Sark.'

Drake caught the eye of a man who was passing the end of his row of stalls towards the saloon, and was beckoned out.

'I will join you after the interval,' he said, turning to Conway, and he saw that his companion was bowing to Miss Le Mesurier.

Miss Le Mesurier in her box noticed Drake's movement, and she asked Mallinson, 'Who is that speaking to Mr. Conway?'

Mallinson put up his glasses and looked. Clarice read recognition in a lift of eyebrows, and guessed from his hesitation to answer who it was that he recognised.

'Well, who is it?'

'Where?' asked Mallinson, assuming an air of perplexity.

'Where you were looking,' said she quietly.

'It's Stephen Drake,' interposed Fielding, and 'Hulloa!' he added in a voice of surprise as he observed the man whom Drake joined.

'Drake! Stephen Drake!' exclaimed Mr. Le Mesurier, leaning forward hurriedly. 'Point him out to me, Fielding.'

The latter obeyed, and Mr. Le Mesurier watched Drake until he disappeared through the doorway, with what seemed to Mallinson a singular intentness. The father's manner waked him to a suspicion that he might possibly have mistaken the daughter's motive in seeking Drake's acquaintance. Was it merely a whim, a fancy, strengthened to the point of activity by the sight of his name in print? Or was it something more? Was there some personal connection between Drake and the Le Mesuriers of which the former was in some way ignorant? He was still pondering the question when Clarice spoke to him.

'So that was the bourgeois, was it?' she said, bending forwards and almost whispering the words. Mallinson flushed.

'Was it?' he asked. 'I can't see. I am rather short-sighted.'

'I begin to think you are.'

The sentence was spoken with an ironic sympathy which deepened the flush upon Mallinson's cheek. A knock at the door offered him escape; he rose and admitted Conway. Conway was received with politeness by Mr. Le Mesurier, with cordiality by his daughter.

'I have Drake with me,' said Conway. 'I came to ask permission, since you invited him to Beaufort Gardens, to introduce him after the next act.'

Mr. Le Mesurier started up in his chair.

'Did you ask him to the house?' he asked Clarice abruptly.

'I asked Mr. Mallinson to bring him,' she replied; and then, with all the appearance of a penitent anxiety, 'Why? Oughtn't I to have done so?' she asked.

Mr. Le Mesurier cast a suspicious glance at his daughter.

'I am so sorry,' she said; 'I didn't know that—'

'Oh well,' interrupted Mr. Le Mesurier hurriedly, 'there's no reason that I know of why you shouldn't have asked him, except that it's surely a trifle unusual, isn't it? You don't know him from Adam.'

'But I assure you, Mr. Le Mesurier,' interposed Conway, 'there's nothing to be said against Drake.'

'Of course!' replied Mr. Le Mesurier, with a testy laugh at the other's warmth. 'We know the length of your enthusiasms, my dear Conway. But I'll grant all you like about Drake. I only say that my daughter isn't even acquainted with the fellow.'

'It is just that drawback which Mr. Conway proposes to remove,' said Clarice demurely. 'Of course,' she went on, 'I should never have thought of inviting him if Mr. Mallinson had not spoken of him so often as his friend.' She directed her sweetest smile to Mallinson. 'You did, didn't you? Yes! Mr. Drake had been away from England for so long that I thought it would be only kind to ask you to bring him. But if I had known that papa had any objection, I should naturally never have done it. I am very sorry. Perhaps I am not careful enough.' She ended her speech in a tone of self-reproach, which had its effect; for her father was roused by it to expostulate.

'My dear,' he said, 'I never hinted that I had an objection to him. You are always twisting people's words and imputing wrong meanings to them.'

Mallinson fancied that he detected a note of something more than mere remonstrance in Mr. Le Mesurier's voice, a consciousness of some thought in his daughter's mind which he would not openly acknowledge her to possess. The perception quickened Mallinson's conjecture into a positive conviction. There was evidently some fact about Drake, some incident perhaps in his life which brought him into relations with the Le Mesuriers,—relations ignored by Drake, but known by Mr. Le Mesurier and suspected by Clarice. Was this fact to Drake's advantage or discredit? The father's manner indicated rather the latter; but Mallinson put that aside. It was more than overbalanced by the daughter's —he sought for a word and chanced on 'forward-ness.' His irritation against her prompted him to hug it, to stamp it on his thoughts of her with a jeer of 'I have found you out.' On the other hand, all his knowledge of her cried out against the word. He looked into the girl's face to resolve his doubts upon the point and found that she was watching him with some perplexity. A question to Conway explained the reason why she was puzzled.

'How did you know that I asked Mr. Drake to Beaufort Gardens?' she asked.

'I was present when Mallinson asked him to go.'

'Mr. Mallinson asked him!' she exclaimed, dropping her fan in her surprise. 'Why, I thought—' She saw the confusion in Mallinson's face and checked herself suddenly with a little laugh of pure enjoyment. Her companion's jealousy was more heroical than she had given him credit for; it had induced him to lie.

To cover his discomfiture Mallinson dived for the fan.

'Oh, don't trouble,' she said, sympathy shaping the words into a positive entreaty. 'You are *so* short-sighted, you know. Then you will bring Mr. Drake,' she turned to Conway as he rose and moved towards the door. Mr. Le Mesurier had resumed his conversation with Fielding, and beyond a slight movement of impatience, he gave no sign that he had heard the words.

'After the next act,' said Conway, and he went out.

Mallinson picked up the fan and laid it upon the ledge of the box.

'I lied to you that evening,' he whispered in a low faltering tone. 'I have no excuse—Can't you guess why I lied?'

There was a feeling behind the words, genuine by the ring of it, and to feeling Clarice was by nature responsive. Mallinson saw the mischief die out of her face, the eyelids droop until the lashes touched the cheek. Then she raised them again, tenderness flowered in her eyes.

'Perhaps,' she said.

She turned from him and watched Conway making his way along the row of stalls. Drake was already in his seat.

'Then why didn't Mr. Drake come if you asked him?' she said with a quick change of tone.

'He gave no reason beyond that it was his first night in London.'

Miss Le Mesurier looked again at Drake. His indifference

irritated her and in a measure interested her in spite of herself. She was not used to indifference, and felt a need to apologise for it to herself. 'Of course,' she reflected, 'he had not seen me then,' and so was reinstated in her self-esteem. The explanation, however, failed her the next moment. For Drake, at all events, had seen her now; she had caught him looking up into the box before Conway left. Yet when Conway communicated his news, Drake never so much as moved his head in her direction. The three blows of the mallet had just sounded from behind the curtain and he sat upright in his seat, his face fixed towards the stage. Clarice bit her lips and frowned.

'Don't be alarmed. He is really quite interested in you.' She looked up. Fielding was standing just behind her shoulder. 'He asked me quite often what you were like.'

'I don't understand you,' said she loftily; and then, 'He might be a schoolboy at his first pantomime.'

'He gives that kind of impression, I believe, in everything he does.'

Miss Le Mesurier had not made the remark in order to elicit eulogy.

'He looks old, though,' she said, and her voice defied Fielding to contradict her.

'Responsibility writes with the cyphers of age,' he quoted solemnly. It was his habit to recite sentences from *A Man of Influence* when Mallinson was present, in a tone which never burlesqued but somehow belittled the work. Mallinson was never able to take definite offence, but he was none the less invariably galled by it.

'As a matter of fact there is hardly a year to choose between the ages of Drake, Conway, and you, Mallinson, is there?' asked Fielding.

Mallinson admitted that the statement was correct.

'He has lived a hard life, has anxieties enough now, I don't doubt. You will find the explanation in that. The only people who remain young nowadays are actors. They keep the child in them.'

The curtain went up as he spoke. As soon as it was lowered again Conway hurried Drake out of the stalls and up the staircase to the box. Clarice welcomed Drake quietly. Mr. Le Mesurier vouchsafed him the curtest of nods.

'Didn't I see you join Israel Biedermann?' asked Fielding. The name belonged to a speculator who had lately been raised into prominence by the clink of his millions.

'Yes,' replied Drake, with a laugh. 'The city makes one acquainted with strange financiers. I have business with him.'

Mr. Le Mesurier showed symptoms of interest.

'Really?' he said. 'You mean to return to Africa, I suppose.'

'If I can help it, no.'

'You intend to stay in England?' asked Mallinson sharply.

'Yes,' replied Drake. He addressed himself to Miss Le Mesurier. 'You were kind enough to invite me to your house on the evening I arrived.'

Mr. Le Mesurier's eyebrows went up at the mention of the day.

'Mr. Mallinson had talked of you,' she explained. 'We seemed to know you already. I saw that you had landed from an interview in the *Meteor*, and thought you might have liked to come with your friend.'

The words were spoken indifferently.

'The *Meteor*?' inquired Mr. Le Mesurier. 'Isn't that the paper which attacked you, Mr. Drake? You let yourself be interviewed by it? I didn't know that.'

He glanced keenly at his daughter, and Mallinson intercepted the look. His conviction was proved certain. There was something concealed, something maybe worth his knowing.

'The attack was of no importance,' replied Drake, 'but I wanted it to be known in some quarters that I had landed without losing time.'

'You replied to the attack?'

'Not so much that. I gave the itinerary of the march to Boruwimi.'

Mr. Le Mesurier perceived his daughter's eyes quietly resting upon him, and checked a movement of impatience, less at the answer than at his own folly in provoking it. Drake turned to Clarice and was offered a seat by her side. He realised, now that she was near, talking to him, that his impression of her, gained from the distance between the box and the stalls, did her injustice. She seemed now the vignette of a beautiful woman, missing the stateliness, perhaps, too, the distinction, but obtaining by very reason of what she missed a counterbalancing charm, to be appreciated only at close quarters, a charm of the quiet kind, diffused about her like a light; winsome—that was the epithet he applied to her,

A. E. W. Mason

and remained doubtfully content with it, for there was a gravity too.

Clarice invited him to speak of Matanga, but Drake was reticent on the subject, through sheer disinclination to talk about himself, a disinclination which the girl recognised, and gave him credit for, shooting a comparing glance at Mallinson.

Mr. Le Mesurier, it should be said, remarked this reticence as well, and it gave him an idea. From Matanga Drake led the conversation back to London, and they fell to discussing the play.

'You are very interested in it,' she said.

'Yes,' said he, 'I have never seen the play before.'

'I should hardly have thought it would have suited your taste,' Conway observed.

'Why? It's French of course, but you can discount the sentiment. There is a stratum of truth left, don't you think?'

Mallinson raised pitying shoulders. 'Of the ABC order perhaps,' he allowed.

'I am afraid it appeals to me all the more on that account,' Drake answered, with a genial laugh. 'But what I meant really was truth to those people—truth to the characters presumed. Consistency is perhaps the better word. I like to see a play run on simple lines to an end you can't but foresee. The taste's barbarian, I don't doubt.'

Miss Le Mesurier's lips instinctively pouted a mischievous 'bourgeois' towards Mallinson. He remarked hastily that he thought the curtain was on the point of rising, and Miss Le Mesurier pushed her opera-glasses towards him with a serene 'Not yet, I think.' Mallinson understood the suggestion of her movement and relapsed into a sullen silence.

By the time that Conway and Drake rose to leave the box Mr. Le Mesurier had thought out his idea. His manner changed of a sudden to one of great cordiality; he expressed his pleasure at meeting Drake, and shook him by the hand, but destroyed the effect of his action through weakly revealing his diplomacy to his daughter by a triumphant glance at her.

At the close of the performance he met Drake in the vestibule of the theatre and lingered behind his party. Fielding, Mallinson, and Conway meanwhile saw Miss Le Mesurier into her carriage.

'What in the world is papa doing?' asked Clarice.

'Exchanging cards with Drake,' replied Fielding. Mallinson turned his head round quickly and beheld the two gentlemen affably shaking hands again. Conway bent into the carriage.

'Do you like him?' he asked.

'Oh yes,' she replied indifferently.

'Then I am glad I introduced him to you,' and some emphasis was laid upon the 'I.'

Mr. Le Mesurier came out to the brougham and the coachman drove off.

'I like that young fellow, Drake,' he said, with a wave of the hand. 'I have asked him to call.'

Clarice did not inform her diplomatic father that unless she had foreseen his intention she would have undertaken the discharge of that act of courtesy herself.

Mallinson took a hansom and drove straight from the theatre to his chambers in South Kensington, Conway walked off in the opposite direction, so that Drake and Fielding were left to stroll away together. They walked across Leicester Square towards St. James's Street, each occupied with his own thoughts. Fielding's were of an unusually stimulating kind; he foresaw the possibility of a very diverting comedy, to be played chiefly for his amusement and partly for Miss Le Mesurier's, by Clarice herself, Drake, and Mallinson. From the clash of two natures so thoroughly different as those of the two men, played off against one another with all the delicate manipulation of Miss Le Mesurier's experienced hand, there was much enjoyment to be anticipated for the purely disinterested spectator which he intended to be. Of the probable *denouement* he formed no conception, and in fact avoided purposely any temptation to do so. He preferred that the play should unroll itself in a series of delightful surprises. The one question which he asked himself at this time was whether Drake might not decline to act his proper and assigned part. He glanced at him as they walked along. Drake looked thoughtful, and was certainly silent; both thought and silence were propitious signs. On the other hand, Drake had interests in the City, had them at heart too, and, worse still, had the City itself at heart.

Fielding recollected an answer he had made to Mallinson. The word 'heart' brought it to his mind. Mallinson was jeering at the journalist's metaphor of the 'throbbing heart' as applied to London. 'The phrase,' Drake had said, 'to me is significant of something more than cheap phraseology. I know that half a throb could create an earthquake in Matanga.' What if the man's established interest in this direction were to suppress his nascent interest in Clarice! Fielding immediately asked Drake what he thought of Miss Le Mesurier.

'Oh!' said the latter, palpably waking from reflections of quite another order, 'I liked her,' and he spoke of her looks.

'She has the art of dressing well,' corrected Fielding, disappointment spurring him to provoke advocacy of the lady. Drake, however, was indifferent to the correction.

'I like her eyes,' he said.

'She is skilled in the use of them.'

'I didn't notice that. They seemed of the quiet kind.'

'At need she can swing a wrecker's light behind them.'

'I like her hand too. It has the grip of a friend.'

'A friend! Yes. There's the pitfall.'

Drake only laughed. He was not to be persuaded to any strenuous defence, and Fielding felt inclined to harbour a grudge against him as needlessly a spoil-sport. Later on, however, when he was in bed it occurred to him that the play might still be performed, though upon different lines, and with a plot rather different from what he had imagined—his plot inverted, in fact. Clarice Le Mesurier, he remembered, had made the first advance to Drake. What if she for once in a while were to figure as the pursuer! That alternative would, perhaps, be the more diverting of the two. He must consult Mrs. Willoughby as to the effect which Drake's bearing would produce on women—consult her cautiously, prudence warned him. Mrs. Willoughby, a cousin and friend of Miss

A. E. W. Mason

Le Mesurier's, was not of the sort to lend a helping hand in the game if the girl was to provide the sport—or indeed in the other event. The one essential thing, however, was that there should be a comedy, and he must see to it that there was one, with which reflection he drew the bed-clothes comfortably about him and went to sleep.

There was, however, one other condition equally essential to his enjoyment, but so apparently inevitable that he did not stop to consider it, namely, that Hugh Fielding should be a mere spectator. It did not occur to him at all that he might be drawn into an unwilling assumption of a part in his own play.

CHAPTER IV

Mallinson on reaching home unlocked a little oak cabinet which hung against the wall beside his writing-table, and searched amongst a litter of newspaper cuttings and incomplete manuscripts. He unearthed at last a copy of the *Meteor*, bought between the Grand Hotel and Beaufort Gardens on the night of Drake's dinner, and, drawing up a chair to the fire, he read through the interview again. The something to be known was gradually, he felt, shaping into a definite form; it had acquired locality this very evening, as he was assured by the recollection of a certain repressed movement upon Mr. Le Mesurier's part at the mention of Boruwimi. Could he add to the knowledge by the help of the interview? Mr. Le Mesurier had not known of its publication until to-night, and so clearly had not read it; his knowledge was antedated. But on the other hand it was immediately after the perusal of the article that Clarice had sent through him her invitation to Drake.

Mallinson studied the article line by line, but without result.

He tossed the newspaper back into the cupboard, changed his coat, and sat down to his writing-table with a feverish impulse to work. He was unable to conceive it possible that Drake should be unaffected by Miss Le Mesurier's attractions. The man was energetic, therefore a dangerous rival. Miss Le Mesurier, besides, seemed bent upon pitting Drake and himself against each other. Why? he asked. Well, whatever the reason, he had a chance of winning—more than a chance, he reflected, remembering a passage of tenderness that evening. His future was promising, if only he worked. Perhaps Clarice only ranged the two men opposite to one another in order to stimulate one of them; he reached an answer to his question 'Why?'

The extravagances of a lover's thoughts have often this much value: they disclose principles of his nature working at the formation of the man, and in Mallinson's case they betrayed his habit of drawing the energy for application from externals, and from no sacred fire within.

He shut his door and worked for a month. At the end of the month, lying in bed at night and watching a planet visible through his window, he saw the ray of light between himself and the star divide into two, and the two beams describe outwards segments of a circle. He turned his face away for a few moments and then looked at the planet again. The phenomenon was repeated. He knew it for a trick of tired eyes and a warning to slacken his labours. On the next afternoon he called at Beaufort Gardens, and was received warmly by Clarice and her aunt.

There was a suggestion of reproach for his long absence in the former's voice, and suggestion of reproach from her kindled him. He explained his plunge under surface on the ground of work. Details were immediately demanded, the plot of the new novel discussed and praised; there was flattery too in the diffident criticism of an incident here and there, and the sweetest foretaste of happiness in the joint rearrangement of the disputed chapter. Mallinson was lifted on a billow of confidence. He was of the type which adjusts itself to the opinions his company may have of him. Praise

Mallinson and he deserved praises; ignore him and he sank like a plummet to depths of insignificance, conscious of insignificance and of nothing more except a dull rancour against the person who impressed the knowledge on him. That way Drake had offended unwittingly at the Grand Hotel; he had recognised no distinction between the Mallinson of to-day and the Mallinson of ten years ago.

Mallinson was asked to dinner on Friday of the next week.

'Really,' said the aunt after his departure, 'he is very clever. I didn't understand what he said, but he is very clever.'

'Yes,' said Clarice reflectively, 'I suppose—I mean of course he is.'

She spoke in a tone of hesitation which surprised her auditor, for hitherto Clarice had been very certain as to her impressions on the point.

At dinner on the following Friday Mallinson was confronted by Conway and had Mrs. Willoughby upon his right. Mallinson liked Mrs. Willoughby, the widow of the black hair and blue eyes, now in the mauve stage of widowhood. She drew him out of the secretiveness within which he habitually barred himself, and he felt thankful to her for his prisoner's hour of mid-day airing. Mrs. Willoughby spoke to Clarice, mentioning a private view of an exhibition of pictures at which she had seen Clarice.

'Who was the cavalier?' she added.

'Mr. Drake,' Clarice replied serenely. 'I met him there by accident.' Mrs. Willoughby looked puzzled, and repeated the name in an undertone.

'You don't know him, I think,' Clarice went on. 'He comes here. Papa asked him to call. Captain Drake, I suppose we ought to call him, but he has dropped the Captain.'

Mrs. Willoughby started and shot a bewildered glance at Mr. Le Mesurier.

'I like the man very much,' said Mr. Le Mesurier, with a touch of championship in his voice. 'You should meet him. I am sure you would like him too.'

Mrs. Willoughby made no answer to the suggestion, and resumed her dinner in silence, while Conway sang his usual paean of praise. After a little she turned to Mallinson.

'Do you know this Mr. Drake?'

'Yes, we were boys together in the same suburb before he went to Africa. It was unfortunately through me that he was asked to this house. I had mentioned him as a friend of mine at one time, and Miss Le Mesurier invited me to bring him on the day he reached London.'

'So soon as that! It's funny Clarice never mentioned him to me. You, of course, told her the date of Mr. Drake's arrival.'

'No, she found that out from an interview in the *Meteor*.'

'I remember.'

'You read it?'

'Yes. So you introduced him to Clarice?'

'No. He did not come that night. Conway brought him up to Mr. Le Mesurier's box when *Frou-Frou* was being played a month ago.'

'Never mind, we will talk of something else.'

Mrs. Willoughby had just observed Clarice. She was nodding assent to the words of her neighbour, but plainly lending an attentive ear to Mrs. Willoughby's conversation. Mrs. Willoughby spoke of indifferent subjects until the ladies rose.

When Mallinson, however, entered the drawing-room, he perceived Mrs. Willoughby's fan motioning him to attendance, and she took up the thread of her talk at the point where she had dropped it.

'You said unfortunately.'

'Well, you have read the *Meteor*.'

'You endorse their view?'

'From what I have seen of Drake since his return, yes.'

'But if there's anything in their charges, why doesn't the Colonial Office move?'

'The Colonial Office!' Mallinson shrugged his shoulders. 'You forget only natives and Arabs were killed in the Boruwimi expedition, and they don't count. If he had killed a white man—What's the matter?'

'Nothing,' said Mrs. Willoughby, recovering from a start; 'an idea occurred to me, that's all.'

'Tell me.'

For a moment Mrs. Willoughby seemed at a loss. Then she said, with a laugh:

'If you will know, I was wondering whether your explanation covered all you meant by "unfortunately."' She lowered her voice. 'You can be frank with me.'

Mallinson was diverted by her assurance of sympathy, and launched out immediately into an elaborate history of the emotions which the friendliness of Miss Le Mesurier to Drake had set bubbling within him. Mr. Le Mesurier approached the pair before Mallinson had finished, and the latter hurriedly broke off.

'Well,' said Mr. Le Mesurier, 'will you meet Mr. Drake, Constance, at lunch, say on Sunday?'

Mrs. Willoughby stared.

'Do you mean that?'

'Certainly.' Mr. Le Mesurier was defiant. Mrs. Willoughby's stare changed to a look of thoughtfulness.

'No,' she said, 'I don't think I could.' She moved away. Mallinson followed her.

'You know something about Drake,' he exclaimed, 'something which would help me.'

'That is hardly generous rivalry,' she replied.

'Does he deserve generosity?' he asked, with a trace of cunning in his expression which Mrs. Willoughby found distasteful.

'If I can help you,' she answered evasively, 'help you honourably, I will,' and she turned away. Mallinson put out a hand to stop her.

'I need help,' he whispered. 'There is a conspiracy to praise the man. You heard Conway at dinner. It's the same with every one, from Mr. Le Mesurier to Fielding.'

'Oh,' she said, her voice kindling to an expression of interest, 'does Mr. Fielding like him? He is fastidious too.' She paused for a second in deliberation, her eyes searching the floor. Raising them, she perceived Mr. Le Mesurier coming towards her.

'I claim our privilege,' she said. 'I will lunch on Sunday, and meet your paragon, after all.'

'I am very glad,' he said impressively. 'Lunch at two.'

Mrs. Willoughby waited until he was out of ear-shot, and turned again to Mallinson.

'It is best that I should see the man, and know something more of him than hearsay. Don't you think so?'

A note of apology discounted the explanation. Mallinson understood that the reference to Fielding was the cause of her change of mind.

'Do you value Fielding's opinion?' he asked.

'Oh, I don't know. On some subjects I think yes. Don't you?'

Mallinson began to wonder immediately whether Fielding's opinions might not be valuable after all, since Mrs. Willoughby valued them. If so, the man might be able to

A. E. W. Mason

throw some light upon other points—for instance, the perplexing question of Miss Le Mesurier's inclinations. Mallinson made up his mind to call upon Fielding. He called on the Sunday morning, and Fielding blandly related to him his history of Sark.

Having worked Mallinson to a sufficiently amusing pitch of indignation, and having hinted his moral that the subjugation of Miss Le Mesurier would be effected only by the raider, Fielding complacently dismissed him and repaired to Beaufort Gardens for lunch. He found Drake upon the doorstep with a hand upon the knocker, and the two gentlemen exchanged greetings.

'I have just left Mallinson,' said Fielding.

Drake's hand fell from the knocker.

'Tell me!' he said. 'Mallinson perplexes me in many ways. For instance, he shows me little good-will now—'

'Does that surprise you?' Fielding interjected, with a laugh.

Drake coloured and replied quickly, 'You didn't let me finish. If he dislikes me, what made him talk about me as his friend to—to the Le Mesuriers before I returned to England?'

'Your name in print. You verged on—well, notoriety. You may laugh, but that's the reason. Mallinson's always on the rack of other people's opinions—judges himself by what he imagines to be their standard of him. Acquaintanceship with a celebrity lifts him in their eyes, he thinks, so really in his own.'

Drake remained doubtfully pondering what credit acquaintanceship with him could confer on any one. He was led back to his old view of Mallinson as a man tottering on a rickety base.

'Will he do something great?' he asked, his forehead puckered in an effort to calculate the qualities which make for greatness.

Fielding chuckled quietly, and answered:

'Unlikely, I think. Clever, of course, the man is, but it is never the work he does that pleases him, but the pose after the work's done. That's fatal.'

Drake looked at Fielding curiously.

'That's a criticism which would never have occurred to me.' He glanced at his watch. 'We have five minutes. Shall we walk round the Gardens?' Fielding chuckled again and assented. He saw the curtain rising on his comedy. For five minutes they paced up and down the pavement, with an interchange of simple questions on Drake's part, and discriminating answers on Fielding's—answers not wholly to encourage, but rather to promote a state of doubt, so much more interesting to the spectator.

When after the five minutes had elapsed they entered the house, they found that Mrs. Willoughby had arrived.

Clarice introduced Stephen Drake to Mrs. Willoughby. He saw a woman apparently in the early twenties, tall, with a broad white forehead, under masses of unruly black hair, and black eyebrows shadowing eyes of the colour of sea-shallows on an August morning. The eyes were hard, he noticed, and the lips pressed together; she bowed to him without a word. Hostility was evidently to be expected, and Drake wondered at this, for he knew Mrs. Willoughby to be Clarice's chief friend and confidante. Mrs. Willoughby fired the first shot of the combat as soon as they had sat down to lunch. She spoke of unscrupulous cruelty shown by African explorers, and appealed to Drake for correction, she said, but her tone implied corroboration.

'I have known cases,' he admitted, 'here and there. You can't always prevent it. The pioneer in a new country doesn't bring testimonials with him invariably. In fact, one case of the kind happened under my own eyes, I might almost say.'

Mrs. Willoughby seemed put out of countenance by Drake's reply. She had plainly expected a strenuous denial of her statement. Drake caught a look of reproof which Mr. Le Mesurier directed towards her, and set it down to his host's courtesy towards his guest. Clarice, however, noticed the look too.

'Indeed,' she said. 'Tell us about it, Mr. Drake. It will be a change from our usual frock-coat conversation.'

Mr. Le Mesurier imposed the interdict of paternal authority.

'I think, my dear, stories of that class are, as a rule, a trifle crude. Eh, Drake?'

Miss Le Mesurier on the instant became personified submission.

'Of course, papa,' she said, 'if you have reason for believing the story isn't suitable, I wouldn't think of asking Mr. Drake to tell it.'

Mr. Le Mesurier raised his hands in a gesture of despair, and looked again at Mrs. Willoughby. His glance said, unmistakably, 'Now see what you've done!' Fielding broke into an open laugh; and Clarice haughtily asked him to explain the joke, so that the others present might share in his amusement.

'I will,' said Fielding. 'In fact, I meant you to ask me to. I laughed, because I notice that whenever you are particularly obedient to Papa, then you are particularly resolved to have your own way.'

Miss Le Mesurier's foot tapped under the table.

'Of course,' she said, with a withering shrug of her shoulders, 'that's wit, Mr. Fielding.' Repartee was not her strong point.

'No,' he replied, 'merely rudeness. And what's the use of being a privileged friend of the family if you can't be rude?'

Drake came to the rescue. 'Mr. Le Mesurier is quite right,' said he. 'Incidents of the kind I mentioned are best left untold.'

'I don't doubt it,' said Fielding. 'A man loses all sight of humanitarian principles the moment he's beyond view of a fireside.'

'Oh, does he?' replied Drake. 'The man by the fireside is apt to confuse sentiment with humanitarian principles; and sentiment, I admit, you have to get rid of when you find yourself surrounded with savages.'

'Exactly! You become assimilated with the savages, and retain only one link between yourself and civilisation.'

'And that link?'

'Is a Maxim gun.'

A. E. W. Mason

'My dear fellow, that's nonsense,' Drake answered in some heat. 'It's easy enough to sit here and discuss humanitarian principles, but you need a pretty accurate knowledge of what they are, and what they are not, before you begin to apply them recklessly beyond the reach of civilisation. When I went first to Africa, I stayed for a time at Pretoria, and from Pretoria I went north in a pioneer company. You want to have been engaged in an expedition of that kind to quite appreciate what it means. We were on short rations a good part of the time, with a fair prospect of absolute starvation ahead, and doing forced marches all the while. When we camped of an evening, I have seen men who had eaten nothing since breakfast, and little enough then, just slip the saddles from the horses, and go fast asleep under the nearest tree, without bothering about their supper. Then, perhaps, an officer would shake them up, and they'd have to go collecting brushwood for fires. That's a pretty bad business in the dark, when you're dead tired with the day's tramp. You don't much care whether you pick up a snake or a stick of wood. I remember, too,' and he gave a laugh at the recollection, 'we used to be allowed about a thimbleful of brandy a day. Well, I have noticed men walk twenty yards away from the camps to drink their tot, for fear some one might jog their elbows. And it was only one mouthful after all—you didn't need to water it. Altogether, that kind of expedition would be something considerably more than an average strain upon a man's endurance, if it was led through a friendly country. But add to your difficulties the continual presence of an enemy, outnumbering you incalculably, always on the alert for you to slacken discipline for a second, and remember you are not marching to safety, but from it. The odds against you are increasing all the time, and that not for one or two days, but for eighty and a hundred. I can assure you, one would hear a great deal less of the harmlessness of the black, if more people had experienced that grisly hour before daybreak, when they generally make their attacks. Your whole force—it's a mere handful—stands under arms at attention in the dark—and it can be dark on the veld, even in the open, on a starlight night. The veld seems to drink up and absorb the light, as though it was so much water trickling on the parched ground. There you stand! You have thrown out scouts to search the country round you, but you know for certain that half of them are nodding asleep in their saddles. For all you know, you may be surrounded on all sides. The strain of that hour of waiting grows so intense that you actually long to see the flash of a scout's rifle, and so be certain they are coming, or to feel the ground shake under you, as they stamp their war-dance half a mile away. Their battle chant, too, makes an uncanny sound, when it swells across the veld in the night, but, upon my soul, you almost hear it with relief.'

Drake stopped and looked round upon faces fixed intently on his own, faces which mirrored his own absorption in his theme. There was one exception, however; Mrs. Willoughby sat back in her chair constraining herself to an attitude of indifference, and as Drake glanced at her, her lips seemed to be moving as though with the inward repetition of some word or phrase. Even Fielding was shaken out of his supermundane quietism.

For the first time he saw revealed the real quality in Drake; he saw visibly active that force of which, although it had lain hitherto latent, he had always felt the existence and understood why he had made friends so quickly, and compelled those friends so perpetually to count with him in their thoughts. It was not so much in the mere words that Drake expressed this quality as in the spirit which informed, the voice which launched them, and the looks which gave them point. His face flashed into mobility, enthusiasm dispelling its set habit of gravity, sloughing it, Fielding thought, or better still, burning through it as through a crust of lava; his eyes—eyes which listened, Fielding had not inaptly described them—now spoke, and spoke vigorously; enthusiasm, too, rode on his voice, deepening its tones—not enthusiasm of the febrile kind which sends the speech wavering up and down the scale, but enthusiasm with sobriety as its dominant note concentrated into a level flow of sound. His description had all the freshness of an immediate occurrence. Compared with the ordinary style of reminiscence it was the rose upon the tree to the dried leaves of a *potpourri*.

'But,' said Fielding, unconsciously resisting the influence which Drake exerted, 'I thought you took a whole army of blacks with you on these expeditions?'

'Not on the one I speak of. In Matanga a small force of them, yes! But even they were difficult to manage, and you could not depend upon them. They would desert at the first opportunity, sell their guns, your peace-offerings of brass rods, and whatever they could lay their hands on, and straggle behind in the dusk until they got lost. It was no use sending back for them in the morning. One would only have found their bones, and their bones pretty well scoured too. I speak of them as a class, of course. There were races loyal enough no doubt, the Zanzibari, for instance. But the difficulty with them was to prevent them fighting when there was no occasion. In fact the blacks who were loyal made up for their loyalty by a lack of common-sense.'

'Cause and effect, I should be inclined to call the combi-nation,' remarked Fielding, 'with the lack of common-sense as the cause.'

Mrs. Willoughby looked her gratitude across the table, and again her lips moved. Drake chanced to catch her eye, and in spite of herself she rippled to a laugh. She had been defending herself by a repetition of the editor's comment of "filibuster."

But at the same moment that Drake's glance met hers she had just waked up to the humour of her conduct, and recognised it as a veritable child's device. She could not but laugh, and, laughing there into the eyes of the man, she lost her hostility to him. However, Mrs. Willoughby made an effort to recover it.

'Well, I don't see,' she said to Drake, 'what right you have got to marching into other people's countries even though they are black.'

'Ah!' Drake answered. 'That's precisely what I call, if I may say so, the fireside point of view. We obey a law of nature rather than claim a right. One can discuss the merits of a law of nature comfortably by a fireside. But out there one realises how academic the discussion is, one obeys it. The white man has always spread himself over the country of the black man, and we may take it he always will. He has the pioneer's hankering after the uttermost corners of the earth, and in addition to that the desire to prosper. He obeys both motives; they are of the essence of him. Besides, if it comes to a question of abstract right, I am not sure we couldn't set up a pretty good case. After all, a nation holds its country primarily to benefit itself, no doubt, but also in trust for the world; and the two things hang together. It benefits itself by observing that trust. Now the black man seals his country up, he doesn't develop it. In the first place he doesn't know how to, and in the second, if he did, he would forget as soon as he could. I suppose that it is impossible to estimate the extent of the good which the opening of Africa has done for an overcrowded continent like Europe; and what touches Europe touches the world, no doubt of that, is there? But I'm preaching,' and he came abruptly to an end.

A. E. W. Mason

'What I don't understand,' said Mr. Le Mesurier, and he voiced a question the others felt an impulse to ask, 'is, how on earth you are content to settle down as a business man in the City?'

Drake retired into himself and replied with some diffidence:

'Oh, the change is not as great perhaps as you think, I have always looked forward to returning here. One has ambitions of a kind.'

'You ought to go into Parliament,' Clarice said.

Drake laughed, thanking her with the laugh. 'It's rather too early to speak of that.'

Mrs. Willoughby observed that he actually blushed. A blushing filibuster! There was a contradiction of terms in the phrase, and he undoubtedly blushed. A question shot through her mind. Did he blush from modesty, or because Clarice made the suggestion?

Mrs. Willoughby asked Fielding for an answer as he stood by the door of her brougham, before she drove away from Beaufort Gardens.

'For both reasons, I should say,' he replied.

'You think, then, he's attracted? He hardly showed signs of it, except that once, and modesty alone might account for that.'

Mrs. Willoughby laid some insistence upon the possibility.

'I should have been inclined to agree with you,' answered Fielding, 'but Drake dragged me round the square before lunch to question me about Mallinson.'

'That makes for your view, certainly. What did you tell him?'

'I painted the portrait which I thought he wanted, picked out Mallinson's vices in clear colours and added a few which occurred to me at the moment. However, Drake closed my mouth with—"He's a hard worker, though."'

'I like the man for that!' cried Mrs. Willoughby, and checked herself suddenly.

'Yes, he's honest certainly.'

'But was he right?'

'Quite! Mallinson works very hard; scents danger, I suppose.'

Mrs. Willoughby heaved a sigh of relief.

'There's some chance for him, then. Will he do anything great?'

Fielding laughed.

'That's one of the questions Drake put to me! I think never.'

Mrs. Willoughby accepted the dictum without asking for the reason. She sat for a moment disconsolately thoughtful. Then she gave a start.

'There's Percy Conway. I had forgotten him!'

'And wisely, I should think. He is just making a back for Drake to jump from if he will.'

'Yes, I noticed that,' said Mrs. Willoughby, with a sneer at the folly of the creature. 'He seems to look upon Mallinson and himself as the two figures which tell the weather in a Swiss clock. When one comes out of his box the other goes in. I catch your trick, you see,' and her face relaxed to a smile.

'Only to improve on it in the matter of truth. For you imply a comparison between Miss Le Mesurier and the weather, and the points of resemblance are strong.'

Mrs. Willoughby's smile became a laugh. 'I don't hold with you about Clarice,' she said. 'You don't know her as I do. She can take things seriously.'

'Intensely so—for five minutes. I have never denied it.'

Mrs. Willoughby did not display her usual alacrity to engage in the oft-repeated combat as to Miss Le Mesurier's merits. Her face grew serious again.

'Does Clarice care for him, you think?'

Fielding was admiring Mrs. Willoughby's eyes at the moment, and answered absently. 'Conway, you mean?'

'No, no! How wilfully irritating you are! This Mr. Drake, of course. By the way, I suppose he will get on?' She spoke in a voice which implied regret for the supposition, and almost appealed for a denial of it.

'I should think there's no doubt of it. They tell me he has just sent a force up country in Matanga to locate concessions. You hit harder than you knew at lunch, for the force carries machine-guns. Oh yes, he'll get on. He has been seen arm-in-arm with Israel Biedermann in Throgmorton Street. You must tell that to a city man to realise what it means.'

'But do you think Clarice cares for him?'

'Miss Le Mesurier cares for—' he began, and broke off with a question. 'Do you read Latin?' He was answered with an exasperated shake of the head. 'Because Miss Le Mesurier always reminds me of an ode of Horace, Finished, exquisite to the finger-tips, but still lacking something. Soul, is it? Perhaps that lack makes the perfection. But what's your objection to Drake?'

Mrs. Willoughby started a little. 'Objection?' she laughed. 'Why? I never told you that I had one.'

'You told not only me, but every one at lunch—Drake himself included.'

Mrs. Willoughby looked doubtfully at Fielding. 'Well,' she said, 'there is something. I feel inclined to explain it to you. You may be able to advise me. Not now!' she went on as Fielding bent forward with a very unusual interest. 'Let me see. Monday, Tuesday, Wednesday'—she ticked off the days upon her fingers. 'Thursday afternoon. Could you come and see me then?'

'Yes.'

'Thanks. Good-bye, and don't forget; five o'clock. I shall be in to no one else.' And Mrs. Willoughby drove off with the smile again upon her face.

CHAPTER V

Whether Fielding was correct in limiting Miss Le Mesurier's capacity for continued seriousness, she was undeniably serious when she called upon Mrs. Willoughby at half-past one on the following day. There were dark shadows under her eyes, and the eyes themselves seemed to look pathetic reproaches at a world which had laid upon her unmerited distress. Mrs. Willoughby was startled at her appearance, and imagined some family disaster.

'Why, Clarice, what has happened?' she exclaimed. 'You look as if you hadn't slept all night.'

Clarice kissed her, and for answer sighed wearifully. Mrs. Willoughby was immediately relieved. The trouble was due, she realised, to some new shuffle of Clarice's facile emotions. She returned the kiss, and refrained from further questions; but, being a practical woman, she rang the bell and ordered the servant to lay two places for lunch.

Clarice sank despondently into the most comfortable chair in the room.

'Not for me,' she said. 'I am sure I couldn't eat anything.'

'You may as well try, dear,' replied Mrs. Willoughby; and

she crossed to Clarice and unpinned her hat—a little straw hat, with the daintiest of pink ribbons. She held it in her hand for a moment, weighing it with a smile which had something of tenderness in it. She laid a light hand upon the brown hair, touching with a caress the curls about the forehead. A child's face was turned up to hers with a pretty appeal of melancholy. Mrs. Willoughby was moved to kiss the girl again. In spite of a similarity of years, she had an affection almost maternal for Clarice; and, with an intuition, too, which was almost maternal, she was able to appreciate the sincerity of the girl's distress, with a doubtful smile at the gravity of its cause.

Clarice threw her arms about Mrs. Willoughby's neck. 'Oh, Connie,' she quavered, 'you can't guess what has happened!' The voice threatened to break into sobs, and there were tears already brimming the eyes.

'Never mind; you shall tell me after lunch.'

At lunch Mrs. Willoughby industriously beguiled her with anecdotes. She talked of an uncle of Clarice, a Philistine sea-captain with pronounced opinions upon the advance of woman, ludicrously mimicking his efforts to adapt a quarter-deck style of denunciation to the gentler atmosphere of a drawing-room. To sharpen his diatribes the worthy captain was in the habit of straining ineffectually after epigrams. Mrs. Willoughby quoted an unsuccessful essay concerning the novels women favoured. 'A woman with a slice of intellect likes that sort of garbage for the same reason that a girl with a neat pair of ankles likes a little mud in the streets.' Clarice was provoked to a reluctant smile by a mental picture of a violent rubicund face roaring the words. She was induced to play with a fragment of sole; she ended by eating the wing of a chicken.

'Now,' said Mrs. Willoughby when she had set Clarice upon a sofa in front of a cosy fire in her boudoir, 'tell me what all the trouble's about.' She drew up a low chair and sat down with a hand upon the girl's arm.

'It's about Sid—I mean Mr. Mallinson,' she began. 'He called yesterday afternoon after you had left. Papa had gone out for a walk, and aunt was lying down with a sick headache. So I saw him alone. He said he was glad to get the opportunity of speaking to me by myself, and he—he—well, he asked me to marry him. He was quite different from what he usually is, else I might have stopped him before. But he made a sort of rush at it. I told him that I was very sorry, but I didn't care for him in that kind of way—at all events yet. And then it was horrible!' The voice began to break again.

Mrs. Willoughby took hold of Clarice's hand, and the latter nestled towards her.

'He got angry and violent, and said that I had persuaded him to give up his profession, and must have known quite well why he did it, and that no woman had a right to interfere with a man's life until she was prepared to accept the responsibility of her interference. I hardly understood what he said, because he frightened me; but I don't think that was at all a nice thing to say, do you, Connie?' and her hand tightened upon her friend's. 'But he said other things too, much worse than that,—I can't tell you. And at last I felt as if I wanted to scream. I should have screamed in a minute or two, I know, so I told him to go away. Then he became silent all at once, and just stood looking at me—and—and—I think that was worse than being abused. At last he said "Good-bye," so sorrowfully, and I knew it would be for ever, and we shook hands, and he went out into the hall and closed the door. It seemed to me that the door would never open again.'

The threatened tears began to fall; Mrs. Willoughby, however, did not interrupt, and Clarice went on.

'So as I heard the front door unlocked to let him out, I opened the door of the room and went into the hall. Mr. Mallinson was standing on the first step. He never looked back—he was turning up his coat-collar—and somehow it all seemed so sad. I felt as if I hadn't a friend left in the world. So—I—I—I—'

'Well?' asked Mrs. Willoughby quickly.

'I called him back into the room, and asked him if we couldn't be friends.'

'What did he answer?'

'That he didn't see how that was possible since he wanted to marry me. But I said that wouldn't matter as long as he didn't tell me so. I think men are so inconsiderate, don't you, Connie?' she broke off in a tone of reproach. 'I can't understand what there is to laugh at. You wouldn't either if you had seen him then, because he just sat down and cried, not as you and I do, you know, but with great tears running through his fingers and heaves of his shoulders. It was heartbreaking. Then he got up and begged my pardon for what he had said, and that was the worst of it all. He declared that if he went the rest of his way alone the journey would be all the easier for the mile I went along with him, and at that somehow I began to cry too, and—and—that's all.'

Mrs. Willoughby sat silent for a little. 'So you refused him,' she said thoughtfully, and she bent towards Clarice. 'Is it to be Stephen Drake?'

Clarice started up from the sofa, and stood looking into the fire. 'What an extraordinary thing that you should ask me that,' she replied slowly, 'because Mr. Mallinson asked it too.' She paused for a second or so and went on. 'I have never thought of him in that way, I am sure. Oh no!' and she roused herself from her attitude of deliberation and crossed to the window, speaking briskly as she went. 'I had quite a different reason.'

Mrs. Willoughby looked at her sharply but said nothing, and presently Clarice turned back into the room as though moved by a sudden impulse. 'Can I write a note here?' she asked.

'Certainly,' replied Mrs. Willoughby, and she set some envelopes and paper on the table. Clarice wrote a few lines and tore them up. She repeated the process on four sheets of note-paper, and as she was beginning the fifth attempt the door was opened and the servant announced that Mr. Conway was waiting in the drawing-room. Clarice tore up the fifth sheet and rose from her chair. 'I can write it when I get home,' she said.

'Percy Conway!' said Mrs. Willoughby when the door was closed again. 'What a funny thing! He's not in the habit of visiting me.'

'The fact is,' said Clarice, without the least embarrassment, as she pinned on her hat, 'I asked him to call for me here. You don't mind, do you?'

'Clarice!' exclaimed Mrs. Willoughby. She stared at the girl, noticing the traces of tears still visible on her face, and then she began to laugh.

'Connie!' said Miss Le Mesurier, and her tone showed that she was hurt. 'You *are* unsympathetic.'

'I can't help it,' cried Mrs. Willoughby, and she laughed yet louder. 'I can't help it, dear!'

'You can't imagine how lonely I have felt since—'

'Since yesterday,' cried Mrs. Willoughby, and her laughter increased. 'Clarice, you'll be the death of me.'

Clarice stood gazing at her patiently, her face grave with reproach, until Mrs. Willoughby succeeded in composing herself to a fitting seriousness. But for all her efforts her mouth worked, and the dimples appeared and vanished in her cheeks, and a little ripple of laughter now and again escaped from her lips.

'Really,' said Clarice, 'I am disappointed in you, Connie.'

'I know it was out of place, dear,' said Mrs. Willoughby with humility, but nevertheless her voice shook as she spoke. Fearing another access she began, as a resource, to lecture Clarice upon the impropriety of making appointments with young gentlemen at other people's houses. The lecture, however, was received with disdain.

'That seems to me still more out of place,' said Clarice.

'Well, we had better go into the drawing-room to Mr. Conway,' said Mrs. Willoughby.

Clarice was indeed excessively indignant with Mrs. Willoughby, for she was in the habit herself of treating her feelings with a tender solicitude, and consequently disliked the want of respect shown to them by her friend. She betrayed the extent of her indignation by a proportionately excessive friendliness towards Conway that afternoon. He was allowed to conduct her to four picture galleries, and a

A. E. W. Mason

Panopticon museum of tortures; his offer to refresh her with tea in Bond Street was shyly accepted, and at parting he was thanked with effusion, 'for the pleasantest afternoon she had spent for some time.'

On reaching home, however, Miss Le Mesurier immediately wrote out the note which she had begun in Mrs. Willoughby's boudoir. She wrote it now without hesitation, as though she had composed the form of its message while in the company of Conway, and addressed it to Stephen Drake. She had a question to ask him, she stated, of some importance to herself. Would he call on Thursday afternoon and answer it? Clarice read through the note before she sealed up the envelope. The word *importance* caught her eye, and she pondered over it for a moment. She crossed it out finally and substituted *interest*. Then she sent her letter to the post. At breakfast on the Thursday morning, Clarice casually informed her father of Drake's visit. 'I wrote to him, asking him to call,' she added.

Mr. Le Mesurier looked up from the pages of his *Times*. 'Why?' he asked quickly.

'I want him to tell me something.'

The *Times* crackled in his hands and fluttered to the floor. He opened his mouth to speak and thought better of it, and repeated the action more than once. Then he scratched his head with a helpless air, and picked up his newspaper. 'Silly girl!' he said at last; 'silly girl!' and relapsed into silence. At the close of breakfast, however, he made an effort at expostulation. 'You will make the man believe you're in love with him,' he said, and in fact he could have chanced on no happier objection to present to her. Clarice flushed to the temples. Sidney Mallinson, Mrs. Willoughby, and now her father! All three had made the same suggestion, and the repetition of it vexed her pride. There were others they might have said it of with more appearance of truth, she thought: Sidney Mallinson himself, for instance, or even Percy Conway. But he, Drake! For a moment she felt inclined to telegraph to him telling him not to come. Then she thought of the motive which had induced her to send for him. No! She would ask her question that afternoon, and so have done with him for good. Aloud she answered:

'How ridiculous! I should hardly think he has that sort of conceit. Anyhow, if he has that impression, I will take care that he does not carry it away.'

Mr. Le Mesurier did not pursue the argument, but he gave certain instructions to his butler, and when Drake arrived at the house he was shown into the library. Mr. Le Mesurier received him.

'Pull up a chair to the fire,' he said with an uneasy geniality. 'I have something to say to you, Drake. It won't take long.'

Drake laid down his hat and seated himself opposite to Mr. Le Mesurier.

'My daughter told me this morning, quite spontaneously, of course, that she had asked you to call in order that she might get from you a certain answer to a certain question, and I thought that I had better prepare you for what that question will be.' He hesitated in his speech, searching for the best way to begin his explanation, and he caught sight of a cigar-box on the mantelshelf above his head.

'By the way, do you smoke?'

'Yes, but I won't just now, thank you.'

'You had better. You can throw it away when I have done. These are in rather a good condition.'

Mr. Le Mesurier seemed inclined to branch off upon the quality of different brands, but Drake gave him no assistance. He lit his cigar and patiently waited, his eyes fixed upon his host. Mr. Le Mesurier felt driven back upon the actual point of his explanation, and almost compelled to fine his words down to just the needful quantity.

'Clarice, I believe,' he said brusquely, 'means to ask you how Gorley died. He was engaged to her.'

Drake did not so much as stir a muscle, even his eyes maintained their steadiness, and Mr. Le Mesurier drew a breath of relief. 'I am glad you take it like this,' he went on. 'I was afraid that what I had to say might have been, well, perhaps a blow to you, and if so the fault would have been mine; for I encouraged you to come here.'

Drake bent forward and knocked the ash off the end of his cigar.

'Yes,' he asked; 'why did you do that?'

Mr. Le Mesurier looked uncomfortable.

'It is only right that I should be frank with you,' he replied. 'The mere fact of Gorley's death, apart from its manner, upset Clarice, more, I confess, than we expected, and made her quite ill for a time. She is not very strong, you know. So it was deemed best, not only by me, but by Gorley's family as well, that she should be kept in ignorance of what had actually happened. We simply told her that Gorley had died near Boruwimi. But I fancy that she suspected we were concealing something. Perhaps our avoidance of the subject gave her the hint, or it may have been Mrs. Willoughby.'

'Mrs. Willoughby?'

'She is related to the Gorley family as well as to us. It was through her Clarice first met Gorley,' he explained, and went on. 'Then you returned to England, and were interviewed in the *Meteor*. Clarice read the interview; you had described in it your march to Boruwimi, and she sent through Mallinson at once an invitation to you. I only found that out the night you were introduced to us at the theatre. It made me certain that she had suspicions, and I admit that I asked you to call in the hope of allaying them. I believed, foolishly as it seems, that if I was cordial, she would give up any ideas she might have, that you were connected in any way with Gorley's death. Afterwards, Drake, I need hardly tell you, I was glad you came here upon other grounds.' Mr. Le Mesurier leaned forward in his chair and touched Drake upon the knee. 'It didn't take long for me to conceive a genuine liking for you, and, of course, I knew all the time that you had only done your duty.'

Drake made no response whatever to Mr. Le Mesurier's sentiment.

'I understand, then,' he said, 'that Miss Le Mesurier was engaged to Gorley at the time of his death?'

'Oh dear, no,' exclaimed the other, starting up from his chair. 'You are aware, I suppose, why Gorley left England?'

Drake nodded assent.

'The engagement was broken off then and there. And Clarice at that time did not seem to take it much to heart. I was inclined to believe that the whole affair had been just a girl's whim. Indeed, in spite of her illness, I am not certain now that that isn't the truth. She may have had some notion of reforming him. I find Clarice rather difficult to understand.'

Drake stood up. 'Where is Miss Le Mesurier?' he asked.

'Upstairs in the drawing-room.'

He took a step towards the door, and took the step unsteadily. He stopped for a second, bracing his shoulders; then he walked firmly across the room. While his hand was on the handle, he heard Mr. Le Mesurier speaking.

'What do you mean to tell her?'

'I hardly understand,' he answered, turning round. 'There surely is but one thing to say—the truth. She has a right to know that.'

'Has she? The engagement was broken off finally when Gorley left England. They had nothing more to do with one another, no common interests, no common future. Has she?'

'It seems to me, yes!'

'We have kept the knowledge from her up till now. No one could blame you if you kept it from her a little longer.'

The argument smacked of sophistry to Drake. He had an unreasoned conviction that the girl had a right to learn the truth from him.

'I think I ought to tell her if she asks me.'

'I might forbid you to do it,' grumbled Mr. Le Mesurier.

'Do you?' asked Drake. The question brought Mr. Le Mesurier up short. It was a direct question, inviting a responsible decision, and Mr. Le Mesurier was averse by nature to making such decisions out of hand. If Drake cared for Clarice, he reflected, it was really in Drake's province to decide the point rather than in his own.

'I don't know enough of you,' he replied, 'to either forbid or give you permission.'

Drake wondered what the sentence meant.

'In that case I must take my own course,' he said, and he went out of the room and mounted the stairs.

A. E. W. Mason

CHAPTER VI

It was the dusk of a February afternoon. Drake had found the lamps lit in Mr. Le Mesurier's library, and the gas was burning in the hall and on the stairs. But within the drawing-room all the light there was came from the fire leaping upon the hearth and from the two recessed windows which faced it. In the farthest of these windows Drake saw Miss Le Mesurier standing, the outline of her face relieved, as it were, against a gray panel of twilight. As the door closed, she turned and took a step into the room. Drake could no longer see more than the shape of her head and the soft waves of hair crowning it; he could not distinguish a single feature, but none the less, as she stood facing him, he felt of a sudden his heart sink within him and his whole strength race out of his body.

Clarice stood still; and he became possessed with a queer longing that she would move again, forwards, within the focus of the firelight. However, she spoke from where she stood.

'You have seen my father.'

Instinctively Drake walked to the fireplace, but she did not follow.

'I have just left him,' he replied. 'He told me what the question was which you wished me to answer.'

'And forbade you to answer it, I suppose?'

'No. He left the choice to me.'

'Well?' she asked.

'I mean to answer it to the full,' he said. 'I was not aware till a moment ago that you had been engaged to Gorley.' Then he hesitated. Clarice was still standing in the shadow, and his desire that she should move out of it and within the circle of light grew upon him until it seemed almost as though the sight of her face and the knowledge of how she was receiving the history of the incident were necessary conditions of its narration.

'I suppose that is the reason,' he went on, 'which made you ask me here at first. Why did you never put the question before?'

'Why?' repeated Clarice slowly, as if she was putting the question to herself. Then she moved slowly towards the fireplace and seated herself by the side of it, bent forwards towards its glow, her elbows upon her knees, her hands propping her chin. Drake gave a sigh of relief, and Clarice glanced at him in surprise, and turned again to the fire. 'Tell me your story,' she said, and left his question unanswered.

Drake began; but now that his wish was accomplished, of a sudden all the reality seemed to fade out of the tragic events he was to recount. His consciousness became in some queer way centred upon the girl who was listening, to the exclusion of the subject she was listening to. He was intensely conscious of her face, of its changing expressions, of the ebb

A. E. W. Mason

and flow of the blood from time to time flushing her cheeks and temples, and of the vivid play of lights and shadows upon them as the flames danced and sank on the hearth. He noticed, too, with an observation new to him, and quite involuntary, the details of the room in which he stood, the white panelling of the walls, the engravings in their frames, the china ranged upon a ledge near to the ceiling. Of these things his mind took impressions with the minuteness almost of a camera. They were real to him at this moment, because they formed the framework and setting of the girl's face and figure.

But Gorley's crime and his expiation of it became by contrast as remote to his apprehension in point of all connection with Clarice as they were in point of locality. He could not realise them to himself as events which had actually happened and in which he had played a part, and he spoke in the toneless voice of one who relates a fable of which, through frequent repetition, he is tired. Instinctively, in order to make the truth of his story palpable, he began to corroborate it with particulars which he would otherwise have spared his auditor, but with the same impersonal accent. He told Clarice of the condition of the village after Gorley's raid, as he first came within view of it: here the body of a negro stood pinned upright against the wall of his hut by an assegai fixing his neck; there another was lying charred upon still-smouldering embers; and as he saw her turn pale and shudder he almost wondered why.

But in spite of his efforts to appreciate its actuality the incident grew more unsubstantial the further he progressed in its narration, and he ended it abruptly.

'Gorley was properly tried,' he said—'his relations testified to the justice of his trial—and he was executed in accordance with the verdict.'

Clarice sat motionless after he had ended. Drake watched the flames sparkle in her gray eyes. At his elbow the clock ticked upon the mantelshelf spacing the seconds, and the fire was hot upon his limbs. That dream-world in Africa dissolved to a vapour.

Clarice recalled him to it at last.

'I never imagined,' she said in a low voice, 'that the truth was anything like this. I shouldn't have asked you if I had. A long time ago I knew that something was being concealed, but I thought it was an accident or—well, I couldn't conceive what it was and I grew curious, I suppose. When you came back to England I thought you might be able to tell me. Lately, however, I began to fancy that you were concerned in it some way. You might have sent Mr.—' she checked herself with the name unspoken and went on, 'you might have sent him on some fatal mission or something of that sort. But this! Oh, why did you tell me?'

She took her hands from beneath her chin and clenched them with a convulsive movement upon her knees. Her memory had gone back to the days when she and Gorley had been engaged, to their meetings, their intimate conversations. This man, in whose hand her hands had lain, whose lips had pressed hers, been pressed by hers, this man had been convicted of a double crime—dastardly murder and dastardly theft—and punished for it! Her pride cried out against her knowledge, and cried out against the man who had vouchsafed the knowledge.

'Why did you tell me?' she repeated, and the words were an accusation.

'You wished to know,' he replied doggedly, 'and it seemed to me that you had the right to know.'

'Right!' she exclaimed, 'right! What right had I to know? What right had you to tell me?'

She rose to her feet suddenly as she spoke and confronted Drake. He looked into her eyes steadily, but with a certain perplexity.

'I felt bound to tell you,' he said simply, and his simplicity appealed to her by its frank recognition of an obligation to her.

'Why,' she asked herself, 'why did he feel bound? Merely because I wished to know the truth of the matter, or because he himself was implicated in it as the instrument of Gorley's punishment?' Either reason was sufficient to appease her. She inclined to the latter; there were conclusions to be inferred from it which staunched her wounded pride.

Clarice turned away. Drake watched her set a foot upon the rail of the fender, lay her hand upon the mantelshelf and support her forehead upon it. After a little she raised her head and spoke with an air of apologising for him.

'Of course,' she said. 'You could not know that there was anything between myself and—and him.'

'No; I could not know that. How should I, for I did not know you? And I am glad that I didn't know.'

Drake spoke with some earnestness, and Clarice looked at him in surprise.

'It would have made my duty so much harder to do,' he explained.

With a little cry of irritation Clarice slipped her foot from the fender and moved from him back to the couch. She had given him the opportunity to escape from his position and he refused to make use of it; he seemed indeed unable to perceive it. However, she clung to it obstinately and repeated it.

'You could not know there was anything between us'; she emphasised the words deliberately. Drake mistook the intention of the emphasis.

'But was there,' he exclaimed, 'at the time? I didn't think of that, Miss Le Mesurier—'

'Oh no, no!' she interrupted. 'Not at the time.' The man was impracticable, and yet his very impracticability aroused in a measure her admiration. 'So you would have shot him just the same, had you known?'

'Shot him?' asked Drake almost absently.

'Yes.'

'Didn't I tell you? I beg your pardon. I didn't shoot him at all. I hanged him.'

Clarice was stunned by the words, and the more because of the dull, seemingly callous accent with which they were spoken.

'You hanged him!' she whispered, dropping the words one by one, as though she was striving to weigh them.

'Yes. I have been blamed for it,' he replied with no change of voice. 'People said I was damaging the prestige of the white man. The argument bothered me, I confess, but I think they were wrong. I should have damaged that prestige infinitely more if I had punished him secretly or—'

'Oh, don't!' she cried, with a sharp interruption, and she stared at him with eyes dilating in horror, almost in fear. 'You can discuss it like that,—the man I had been engaged to,—you hanged him!'

She ended with a moan of actual pain and covered her face with her hands. On the instant Drake woke to a full comprehension of all that he had said, and understood something of the humiliation which it meant to her.

Clarice was sitting huddled in her chair, her fingers pressed lightly on her eyes, while now and again a shiver shot through her frame.

'Still I was bound to tell her,' Drake thought. He waited for a little, wondering whether she would look up, but she made no movement. An emerald ring upon her finger caught the light and winked at him maliciously, leering at him, he fancied. There was nothing more for him to say, and he quietly went out of the room.

The click of the door-handle roused Clarice. She saw that the room was empty, and, drawing a breath of relief, started out of her chair. Standing thus she heard Drake's footsteps descending the stairs, and after a pause the slamming of the hall-door. Then she went to the fireplace and knelt down close to it, warming her hands at the blaze.

'The degradation of it!' she whispered.

CHAPTER VII

Bit by bit she sought to reconstruct the scene, piecing it together out of Drake's words; but somehow that scene would not be reconstructed. She gradually found herself considering Drake's words as a light thrown upon the man who spoke them, rather than as the description of an actual incident. The humiliation which she experienced made her shrink with a certain repulsion from her recollections of Gorley and dwell instead upon the contrasting tones in Drake's voice, the contrasting expressions upon his face when he spoke to her and when he merely narrated his story. In the first instance gentleness had been the dominant characteristic, in the second indifference; and that very indifference, while it repelled her, magnetised her thoughts.

Something indeed of the same process which had caused that appearance of indifference in Drake was now repeating itself in Clarice. Drake was superseding Gorley in her mind. She struggled against the obsession and morbidly strove to picture to herself the actual execution: the black troops ranged in a clearing before the smouldering village, looking up at one figure—Gorley's—spinning on a rope. But even upon that picture Drake's face obtruded. She thrust out her hands to keep it off, as though it was living and pressing in upon her; for a moment she tried to conjure up Gorley's face, but it was blurred—only his form she could see spinning on

A. E. W. Mason

a rope, and Drake beneath it, his features clear like an intaglio and firm-set with that same sense of duty which had forced him sternly to recount to her the truth that afternoon. She recurred to her recent habit of comparing him with Mallinson. She had a vision of Mallinson, with the same experience to relate,—if that were imaginable—fidgeting through evasions, grasping at any diversion she might throw out for him to play with.

But what if Drake's frankness, outspoken to the point of cruelty, sprang from an indifference to her? Clarice had seen a good deal of Drake lately. She caught herself almost smiling at the idea, softening at its palpable falsity. In a last effort at resistance she fixed her thoughts on the cruelty, the callousness, in his method of narration, and began to feel herself on solid ground. She was consequently inspired to run over all that he had said, in order to make her footing yet firmer, and at the outset she was brought to a check. Why had she never questioned him upon the matter before? he had asked. Clarice stopped and asked the question of herself. At the beginning of their acquaintance certainly there had always been others by, but afterwards there had been opportunities enough. But by that time, what with her father's and Mrs. Willoughby's hostility, she had begun to suspect that Drake was in some way implicated in the mystery. Was it because she was afraid to know it for certain that she had refrained? She recalled her letter to him written last Monday, and how she had crossed out 'importance' and substituted 'interest.' Was this knowledge important to her, really important, bearing issues in the future? It could only be important, she realised, if she set great store upon her acquaintanceship with Drake. Drake, in fact, had achieved something of a triumph, though quite unknown to himself, for he had compelled Clarice Le Mesurier to abandon the consideration of his attitude towards her in favour of a search after the state of her feelings towards him.

She was still engaged in the search when the clock struck six, and, rousing herself brusquely, she rang the bell for the lamps to be brought.

At that moment Mrs. Willoughby had just finished telling to Fielding the story which Drake had told to Clarice.

'So that's what Drake was referring to on Sunday,' said Fielding.

'Yes,' said Mrs. Willoughby.

'What in the world made you attack him in that way, if you didn't want Clarice to suspect?'

'The fact was, I was a fool, I suppose. I just put my head down and charged. But what I want your advice upon is this, ought Clarice to be told now—before things go further?'

'No, no!' said Fielding. He saw the curtain descending precipitately upon his comedy before the climax was reached, and he added quite sincerely, 'I like Drake. I don't see why he shouldn't have a run for her money.'

Mrs. Willoughby looked doubtful for a moment, and then she said, 'Very well.' She hesitated for a second: 'I think I like him too.'

A. E. W. Mason

CHAPTER VIII

This was by no means the last occasion upon which Mrs. Willoughby thought it prudent to take counsel with Fielding concerning the affairs of her friend. Nor was Fielding in any degree backward to respond with his advice. He developed, in fact, an interest in their progress quite disproportionate to his professed attitude of the spectator in the stalls. Mrs. Willoughby lived at Knightsbridge, in a little house, of which the drawing-room overlooked the Park close to the barracks, and he found it very pleasant to sit there of an afternoon and discuss in a cosy duet the future of Clarice.

The subject, besides, had the advantage of inexhaustibility. On the one side Fielding ranged the suitors, or those whom he considered such; on the other the vagaries of the girl. Playing these forces off not merely against each other, but against themselves as well—for, as he pointed out, there was no harmony in the separate camps—he evolved an infinite number of endless complications. There was consequently no end to the discussion, not even when Clarice was argued through the marriage ceremony. For that point Fielding took to represent the one o'clock in the morning of a carnival ball; then the fun really begins, though decent people have to go away.

Mrs. Willoughby was, as ever, staunch in her defence,

though a recollection of Clarice's tearful visit with Conway's arrival for a climax prompted her now and again to laugh in the midst of it.

'You mistake thoughtlessness for tricks,' she said. 'Clarice is only a child as yet.'

'She has a child's capacity for emotion, I admit,' corrected Fielding, 'but a woman's knowledge of its use. The combination is deplorable.'

Fielding inquired about Drake, and was told that he had not been seen lately. 'It looks as if he was declining in favour,' Mrs. Willoughby added.

'Not necessarily. The man's busy—there's a company coming out.'

'A solid one?'

'Likely to be, since Drake handles it. I am thinking of taking shares.'

Mrs. Willoughby was surprised. Fielding seemed to her the last man calculated by nature for dabbling in stocks.

'You!' she exclaimed. Fielding nodded assent.

'Then don't do it,' Mrs. Willoughby flashed out vigorously. 'Don't think of it. Oh, I know those men in the City! Their friends get ruined, and they—well, I mustn't say anything against them, because my husband was one of them, poor dear,—but they move into larger offices. Mr. Drake has been asking you to join him?'

'He hasn't done anything of the sort. I heard of the matter

through quite an independent channel. However, I am not ruined yet, and the company won't be floated for another four months. And, after all, it's my money.'

Mrs. Willoughby became quiet.

'Well,' she said, and she derived some satisfaction from the thought, 'at all events Clarice has dropped talking about him.'

Fielding laughed.

'That means that it's Mallinson's turn on the roundabout and nothing more.'

'Sidney Mallinson has been refused.'

'Refused! When?'

'On the Sunday we lunched at Beaufort Gardens.'

'Oh!'

Fielding was silent for a moment. He was thinking that he had met Mallinson of late with unusual frequency here at Mrs. Willoughby's house.

'But are you sure?' he asked.

'Certain; he told me so himself. Clarice told me too the day after.' Mrs. Willoughby began again to laugh. 'She would have prevented him if she could, but apparently he tried to take her by storm.'

'Oh!' exclaimed Fielding. 'On the Sunday afternoons you say? Then I was to blame, I am afraid, for I gave him precisely that advice on the Sunday morning. Of course, I never thought that he would take it.'

Fielding met Sidney Mallinson again and again at the house in Knightsbridge. He was invited to dinner, but so was Mallinson, and the latter had confidential talks with Mrs. Willoughby. He dined with some friends at the Savoy and went on in a comfortable frame of mind to a concert; there Mrs. Willoughby joined them, so did Mallinson, and the couple sat side by side and conversed through a song. 'The height of bad taste,' commented Fielding in an access of irritation. The fellow was spoiling his comedy by relinquishing his part. He drew Mallinson aside as they passed through the hall.

'You seem to see a good deal of Mrs. Willoughby?'

'Yes, we generally pair off together.'

Fielding dropped plump among the coarse sensations of the ordinary human. He wanted to kick Mallinson, and to kick him hard. He saw with an anticipatory satisfaction the glasses flying off the supercilious gentleman's nose, and felt the jar at the end of his boot as it dashed into the coat-tails. The action would have been too noticeable, however, and he only said, 'What a very *bourgeois* thing to do!'

Mallinson's air of complacency vanished as he heard the offensive term levelled against himself. He did not, however, on that account change his attitude towards Mrs. Willoughby. Fielding found him at the house a few days later, and proceeded to sit him out. The contest drove Fielding to the last pitch of exasperation, for, apart from the inherent humiliation of the proceeding, Mrs. Willoughby was directly encouraging Mallinson to stay.

Mallinson at last was suffered to leave, and Mrs. Willoughby, instead of resuming her seat, walked across to the window and scrutinised intently the passers-by.

'That creature visits you pretty often, it appears,' said Fielding.

'Does he?' she asked. 'He comes to me for the sake of consolation, I suppose.'

'And makes love to you for the sake of contrast. He tells me you generally pair off together when you meet. Pair off!' and he grimaced the phrase to show how little he minded it. 'It'll be "keeping company" next.'

Mrs. Willoughby gave a little quiet laugh. Her back was towards him, so that he could not catch her expression, but she seemed to him culpably indifferent to the complexion which Mallinson had given to their friendship.

'It's rather funny,' she said, 'though I can't help feeling sorry for him.'

'I saw that you were sorry for him,' Fielding interrupted.

'But he pretends,' Mrs. Willoughby went on, ignoring the interruption with complete unconsciousness—'he pretends to himself that I am Clarice. He talks to me as if I were. He called me "Clarice" the other day, and never noticed the mistake, and that's not my name, is it?' She turned to him quite seriously as she put the question.

'No,' replied Fielding, 'your name's Constance,' and he dwelt upon the name for a second.

'Yes—Constance,' said Mrs. Willoughby thoughtfully. 'It sounds rather prim, don't you think?'

'Constance,' Fielding repeated, weighing it deliberately. 'Constance—no, I rather like it.'

'Clarice shortens it to Connie.'

'Does she indeed? Connie—Constance.' Fielding contrasted the two names, and again, 'Constance—Connie.'

Mrs. Willoughby's mouth began to dimple at the corners.

'Although one laughs,' she proceeded, 'it's really rather serious about Mr. Mallinson. He told me once the colour of my eyes was—'

'Do you let him talk to you about the colour of your eyes?' Fielding was really indignant at the supposition.

'He didn't ask my permission,' Mrs. Willoughby said penitently. 'But it isn't a thing people ought to do. He said they were gray, and they aren't, are they?' She turned her face towards him.

'Gray? Of course not,' said Fielding, and starting from his chair, he approached Mrs. Willoughby at the window to make sure.

'Clarice's are, I know, but I am certain mine aren't.' She held up her face towards the light, and the remark was pitched as a question.

'Yours,' said Fielding, examining them, 'Neptune dipped them in the sea at six o'clock on an August morning.'

Mrs. Willoughby moved away from the window precipitately. 'So, if Mr. Mallinson is so fond of Clarice,' she said, 'that he sees her in everybody one can't help pitying him.'

Mrs. Willoughby, however, for a short time subsequently was not seen in the company of the discarded lover, and Fielding inferred with satisfaction that her pity was taking a less active form. He was roused to a perception that his inference was false one night at the opera.

Mrs. Willoughby was present with Mr. Le Mesurier and Clarice. Percy Conway he hardly reckoned, counting him at this time, from his constant attendance, rather as an item of Clarice's toilette; and Fielding took care to descend the staircase after the performance in close proximity to the party.

'And how's Mr. Mallinson?' he asked of Mrs. Willoughby, not without a certain complacency in his voice.

'Oh, poor boy!' she replied with the tenderest sympathy, 'he's in bed, ill.'

'Ill?' asked Clarice quickly. 'You don't mean that.'

'Yes. I'm so concerned. He wrote to tell me all about it.'

Fielding looked displeased, and much the same expression was to be seen on the face of Clarice. Mrs. Willoughby was serenely unconscious of the effect of her words.

'I heard that he was in bed,' interposed Conway carelessly. 'But apparently he has got something to console himself with.'

'Yes. He wrote to me about that too,' said Mrs. Willoughby. 'Fancy, Clarice! He has inherited quite a good income. An uncle or somebody left it to him.'

Clarice expressed an acid satisfaction at the news. She

dropped behind with Fielding.

'You didn't know that Mr. Mallinson was ill?' she asked. 'Did none of his friends know except Connie?' and then there was a perceptible accent of pique in her voice.

Fielding did not answer the question immediately. He had been brought of a sudden to the vexatious conclusion that Mrs. Willoughby was a coquette just like the rest of her trivial sex—no better, indeed, than the girl at his side, whose first anxiety was not as to whether Mallinson was seriously ill, but why he wrote the information to Mrs. Willoughby. He felt that Mrs. Willoughby had no right to trifle with Mallinson. The poor fellow had already suffered his full share of that kind of experience.

Miss Le Mesurier repeated her question impatiently, and Fielding suddenly realised that Miss Le Mesurier's pique might prove useful in setting matters right. He determined to encourage it.

'None that I'm aware of,' he replied. 'Mrs. Willoughby, of course, would be likely to know first.'

'Why?'

'Haven't you noticed? They have struck up a great friendship lately—always pair off together, you know.'

Miss Le Mesurier's lips curled at the despicable phrase, but she blamed Mrs. Willoughby for the fact which it described, not Sidney Mallinson. His attitude she could understand, and make allowance for; it had been a despairing act prompted by an instinct of self-preservation to rid himself of the hopeless thought of her. An unsuccessful act too, for the poor fellow had broken down. She had no doubts as to the

A. E. W. Mason

origin of his illness, and overflowed promptly with sympathy. Her resentment against Mrs. Willoughby none the less remained.

Driving homewards she asked her, 'Why didn't you tell me before that Mr. Mallinson was ill?'

'My dear, I never gave a thought to it until I saw Mr. Fielding. The illness isn't serious,' and Mrs. Willoughby laughed, with peculiar heartlessness thought Clarice. They were, however, not thinking of the same individual.

Mrs. Willoughby, Clarice, and Fielding in consequence suffered some such change in their relative positions as is apt to take place amongst the European Powers. Poor Mrs. Willoughby, in the innocent pursuit of her own ideas, had suddenly roused two former friends into a common antagonism. These friends, besides, had much the same grounds for resentment as the Powers usually have, for Mrs. Willoughby's conduct was a distinct infringement of rights which did not exist. Clarice and Fielding drew perceptibly nearer to one another; they exchanged diplomatic *pourparlers*. Fielding found a great deal to praise in Mallinson, and Clarice had a word or two to say upon the score of widows. She was doubtful whether they ought ever to re-marry. Fielding kept an open mind on the subject, but was willing to discuss it. On the particular point, however, whether this widow was to marry Mallinson they were both uncompromisingly agreed, and were only hindered from an armed demonstration by the suspicion that the sinner to the overawed would merely laugh at it. On the whole Fielding deemed it best to address a friendly remonstrance to Mrs. Willoughby in the interests of Clarice. He suggested that she should see less of Sidney Mallinson.

'But I have no grounds for slamming my door in his face,'

she answered plaintively. 'You see, Clarice has refused him, and really he's very sweet and polite to me.'

Fielding pointed out with the elaborate calmness of intense exasperation that there could be no finality in a refusal given by Miss Le Mesurier. Mrs. Willoughby replied that they had differed before in their views of Clarice, and that the point he mentioned was one upon which Mr. Mallinson must be left to judge for himself. 'Exactly,' said Fielding with emphasis, 'he should be left to judge for himself,' and was for marching off with colours flying. But Mrs. Willoughby could not refrain from declaring that the unprecedented interest which Mr. Fielding took in his friend Mr. Mallinson had raised that friend to a very different position in her esteem from that which he had held before.

The combat was renewed more than once, but with no different result, and upon the same lines. Mrs. Willoughby received his attacks with a patient humility, and rushed out to catch him a flout as he was retiring. Finally, however, she shifted her position, and became the aggressor. She suggested that Fielding was really in love with Clarice, and trying to gain favour with her by bringing an admirer back to her feet. Fielding was furious at the suggestion, and indignantly repudiated it. She ignored the repudiation, and quietly insisted in pointing out the meanness of such a system of making love. The unfortunate gentleman's dignity constrained him to listen in silence, for he felt that he would have spluttered had he opened his lips. The only course open to him was a retreat with a high head, and he declared that it was no longer possible for him to continue a discussion which he had begun as much in her true interests as on behalf of justice and her particular friend Miss Le Mesurier, and went home. By return of post he received a pen-and-ink drawing of himself and Clarice 'pairing off.' He was figured in the costermonger's dress, with his arm tucked under the girl's, and her hat on his head.

Meanwhile Mallinson was still in bed, completely ignorant of the battle which had been waged for the possession of him.

Fielding thought more than once of calling at his flat, since his determination had been sharpened rather than overcome by the victories of Mrs. Willoughby. He was more than ever convinced that Mallinson ought to have a fair chance with Miss Le Mesurier—an equal chance with Drake. The name of Drake made him pause. Miss Le Mesurier knew everything there was to be known about Mallinson, but there were certain facts in Drake's history of which she was ignorant. The question sprang into his mind, 'Could Mallinson have a fair chance unless she was made acquainted with those facts?' Fielding knew Members of Parliament who had been returned over the heads of residents in the constituency because they entered it too late for the electors to become intimate with their defects. Drake's career might provide an analogy unless Clarice was told. He argued to convince himself that he felt she ought to be told, but he could not bring himself to the point of telling. He decided finally upon an alternative which would, he imagined, secure his purpose, while relieving him of the responsibility. He would tell Mallinson of the Gorley episode, for the rival surely had a right to know. Whether Clarice was to be informed or not, Mallinson should be allowed to judge.

Fielding assured himself of the justice of his intention for the space of two days without putting it into execution, but on the third he chanced to meet Conway, and was given the information that Mallinson's inherited income amounted to a thousand pounds. The news decided him. Under these circumstances Mallinson certainly ought to know. He jumped into a hansom and drove down to South Kensington.

Mallinson was still in bed, but sufficiently recovered to write up his diary. The book lay upon the counterpane open, but as Fielding was introduced into the room, its author shut it up and tucked it under his pillow. It was kept entirely for his own perusal, a voluminous record of sensations ranging from a headache to a fit of anger, without the mention of an incident from cover to cover.

'I hear you have had a touch of bronchitis,' said Fielding.

'Something more than a touch, I can tell you. I have been rather ill. However, I am going to get up to-morrow.'

Fielding found it difficult to come to the point of his visit.

'You must have found it dull.'

'Not very. I can always interest myself. Drake came to see me yesterday.'

'Drake! How did he know? Conway told him, I suppose.'

'No, Miss Le Mesurier told him.'

'Miss Le Mesurier?' he asked.

'Yes. Are you surprised?' The question was put with some resentment.

'That she told him? No, I expect she sent him.' A smirk upon the invalid's face showed he shared the thought.

'By the way,' Fielding continued, 'talking of Miss Le Mesurier, did you ever meet a man called Gorley?'

'No. There was a Gorley who was engaged to her. Is that

the man?'

'Yes. I heard rather a strange story about him. He went out to Africa, you know.'

Mallinson lifted himself on his elbow.

'Africa,' he said slowly. 'Yes, I heard that. Why do you mention him?'

'Oh, I thought perhaps you might have known the man, that's all. He's dead.'

Fielding spoke with a studied carelessness, looking anywhere except at Mallinson.

'Dead,' repeated Mallinson in the same tone, but his heart was beginning to race, and he lifted himself higher into a sitting position. 'Gorley was a relation of Mrs. Willoughby, I believe.'

'A kind of cousin.'

There was silence between the men for a second or two. Mallinson was recalling what Mrs. Willoughby had said that evening at Beaufort Gardens, when Mr. Le Mesurier pressed her to meet Stephen Drake at lunch.

'So Gorley died in Africa,' he remarked. 'Where? Do you know?'

'Yes; at Boruwimi.'

Mallinson started. Fielding glanced at him involuntarily, and their looks crossed.

'A strange story, you said. Suppose you tell it me. It will while away some of my time.'

Fielding lit a cigarette and related the story. At the end of it Mallinson lay back on the pillows, staring at the ceiling. Once or twice Fielding spoke to him, but he did not hear. He was not thinking: the knowledge that the secret to be discovered was his to use was as a sense in him. He felt it pulsing through his veins and throbbing at his heart. Mrs. Willoughby was forgotten. It had been after all but a fictitious fancy which he had conceived for her, a fancy fostered in the main as balm for his self-respect after his refusal by Clarice.

As soon as he was sufficiently recovered he called upon Miss Le Mesurier, confident that his hour and opportunity had come. Drake, however, had reported to Clarice on the condition of Mallinson, and her sympathy had in consequence to a great extent evaporated. Bronchitis was not of the ailments which spring from a broken heart, and she was inclined to hold it as a grievance against him that she had been so wastefully touched with pity. Her sympathy disappeared altogether when with little circumlocution he broached the subject of the Boruwimi expedition, and dropped a mention of Mrs. Willoughby's relative. There was something at the back of it, he hinted.

Clarice wondered whence he had got his information, but made no effort to check him. She stood looking out of the window while he retold her the story of Gorley's death. It became more unreal to her than ever; for while his account was correctly given, as Mrs. Willoughby had given it to Fielding, it lacked the uncompromising details which Drake himself had furnished. Her recollection of these details made the man who had given them stand out in her thoughts.

A. E. W. Mason

'It was a pitiful affair,' Mallinson concluded, 'but I thought you ought to know.'

Clarice drew a finger down the frame of glass in front of her.

'Mr. Drake thought so too,' she said quietly.

'Drake!' exclaimed Mallinson, utterly bewildered. 'Drake! The man wouldn't be such a—'

'He was though.'

'Do you mean that he confessed to it?'

'Confess?' she said, turning towards him. 'That is hardly the word. He told me of his own accord the moment he knew I had been engaged to—to—' She broke off at the name, and continued, 'and he spared himself in the telling far less than you have spared him.'

She spoke with a gentle dignity which Mallinson had never known in her before, and he felt that it raised a more solid barrier between them than even her refusal had done.

Fielding, meanwhile, waited with an uneasy conscience which no casuistry would lighten. He threw himself in Mallinson's way time after time in order to ascertain whether the latter had spoken. Mallinson let no word of the matter slip from him, and for the rest seemed utterly despondent. Fielding threw out a feeler at last.

'Of course,' he said, 'you would never repeat what I told you about Gorley. I forgot to mention that.'

Mallinson flushed. 'Of course not,' he said awkwardly.

Fielding turned on him quickly. 'Then what made you tell Miss Le Mesurier?'

Mallinson was too taken aback to deny the accusation. 'Oh, Miss Le Mesurier,' he replied, 'knew already.'

'She knew? Who told her?'

'Drake.'

Fielding drew in his breath and whistled. His first feeling was one of distinct relief, that after all he had not been the means by which Clarice had come to her knowledge; his second was one of indignation against Drake. He realised how a frank admission from Drake would outweigh in the girl's susceptible nature the fact admitted. 'What on earth induced him to reveal it?'

'I suppose he is a little more cunning than one took him for. No doubt he saw the thing would get known sooner or later, and thought the disclosure had better come from himself.'

Fielding had been leaning to the same opinion, but the moment he heard it stated, and stated by Mallinson, he felt a certain conviction that it was wrong. 'I don't believe that,' he said sharply.

He was none the less, however, indignant with Drake. To intermeddle at all in other people's concerns was averse to his whole theory of existence. But to intermeddle, and not very creditably, and out of the most disinterested motives of benevolence and expediency, and then to fail! All this was nothing short of degrading. He dined that night at his club, to which Drake had been elected, and lay in wait for him. Drake, however, did not appear, and at ten o'clock Fielding went round to his rooms.

A. E. W. Mason

Drake was living in chambers on the Embankment, a little to the west of Hungerford Bridge. As he was shown into the room, Fielding could not help noticing the plainness of its furniture and adornment. The chairs were covered with a cheap red cretonne; there was an armchair or two with the high seat and long elbows, which seemed to have gone astray from a Peckham drawing-room; an ormolu clock under a glass shade ornamented the overmantel, and in the way of literature there was one book in the room—Prescott's *Conquest of Peru*—and a copy of the *Times*.

Drake was seated at the table engaged in the study of a map of Matanga. 'Come in!' he said cordially. Fielding drew up a chair to the fire. 'Have a drink? The cigars are on the mantelshelf.'

Drake fetched a syphon and a decanter of whisky and mixed two glasses. He handed one to Fielding, and brought his map to the fire.

'Ah!' said Fielding. 'There's likely to be a rising in Matanga, I see.'

'Very possibly.'

'How will that affect you?'

'Not at all, I think. It may delay things, of course, but it won't take long, and, besides, it won't touch the interior of the country. There will be a certain amount of shouting in the capital and round the coast, perhaps a gun or two fired off, and then they'll settle down under a new President.'

'But there are a good many Germans there, aren't there? What if they invite the German Government to interfere?'

'I don't fancy that's probable. The German colonist isn't over fond of German rule. You see the first thing a German official wants to do when he catches sight of a black, is to drill him. It's his first and often his last idea. He wants to see him holding the palm of his hand against the stripe of an invisible trouser, and the system doesn't work, because the black clears over the nearest border.'

Fielding laughed and turned to the object of his visit. 'Talking of Matanga, what in the world made you tell Miss Le Mesurier about Gorley?'

Drake looked up from his map. 'How did you know anything about Gorley?' he asked.

'Mrs. Willoughby told me. I thought it was decided Miss Le Mesurier should not be told.'

'Mr. Le Mesurier left the choice to me, and it seemed to me that she had a right to know.'

'Why?'

Drake paused for a second in reflection. 'It seemed to me—' he began again.

'Well, she hadn't,' snapped Fielding.

'Well, I think she had,' answered Drake quietly, returning to his map.

'Then you were wrong; she hadn't. The engagement was broken off a long while ago, and you hadn't a right to tell her unless you want to marry her yourself.'

Drake raised his head with a jerk and stared at the wall in

front of him fixedly. He made no answer, nor could Fielding distinguish upon his face any expression which gave a clue to his thoughts. He got up from his chair, and Drake turned to him. 'I gather from your tone,' he said in an indifferent voice, 'that Mrs. Willoughby resents my action.'

'My dear fellow, no,' exclaimed Fielding energetically. 'For Heaven's sake, don't take me for a reflex of Mrs. Willoughby!'

No more plotting for him, he determined. He had planned and calculated and interfered, all for other people's good, and this was the thanks he got; to be quietly informed that he hadn't an idea of his own.

The next afternoon Mrs. Willoughby stopped her phaeton beside him in Bond Street. She looked very well, he thought, with her clear complexion,—clear as those clear eyes of hers with just the hint of azure in the whites of them—wind-whipped now to a rosy warmth.

'May I congratulate you yet?' she asked pleasantly.

Fielding was not to be provoked to renew the combat, and he put the question aside. 'You remember what you told me the other day about Gorley,' he said.

'Yes,' she answered, becoming serious.

'Well, Miss Le Mesurier knows.'

'Who told her?' and she leaned forward.

'Guess.'

Mrs. Willoughby thought for a moment and then shook her

head. 'I can't. Her father?'

'No; Drake himself.'

She started back in her seat. Then she said, 'Of course, we might have known that he would,' and the 'we' sealed their reconciliation.

A. E. W. Mason

CHAPTER IX

When Fielding had gone, Drake opened the window and stepped out on the balcony.

'Unless you want to marry her yourself'; the words were stamped upon his mind in capitals. They formulated to him for the first time the cause of that unreasoned conviction of his, and formulated it too, as he realised, with absolute truth. Yes, it was just his desire for Clarice to which he owed his belief that she had an unquestionable right to know his responsibility for Gorley's death.

He wanted her, and wanting her, was committed to scrupulous frankness.

Drake looked out across the city. At his feet lay the quiet strip of garden, lawn and bush; beyond, the lamps burning on the parapets of the Embankment, and beyond them, the river shining in the starlight, polished and lucent like a slab of black marble, with broad regular rays upon it of a still deeper blackness, where the massive columns of Hungerford Bridge cast shadows on the water. An engine puffed and snorted into the station, leaving its pennant of white smoke in the air. Through the glass walls of the signal-box above the bridge Drake could see the men in a blaze of light working at the levers, and from the Surrey end there came to him a clink, and at that distance a quite musical clink, of truck against truck as some freight-train was shunted across the rails. Away to his right the light was burning on Westminster clock-tower; on Westminster Bridge the lamps of cabs and carriages darted to and fro like fire-flies. Drake watched two of them start across in the same direction a few yards apart, saw the one behind close up, the one in front spirt forward as though each was straining for the lead. They drew level, then flashed apart, then again drew level, and so passing and repassing raced into the myriad lights upon the opposite bank. That bank was visible to him through a tracery of leafless twigs, for a tree grew in front of his window on the farther edge of the gardens, and he could see the lights upon its roadway dancing, twirling, clashing in the clear night, just as they clashed and twirled and danced in the roadway beneath him, sparks from a forge, and that forge, London. In their ceaseless motion they seemed rivulets of fire, and the black sheet of water between them the solid highway. But even while he looked, a ruby light moved on that highway out from the pillars of the bridge, and then another and another. Everywhere was the glitter of lights; fixed, flashing like a star on the curve, or again growing slowly from a pin's point to an orb, and then dwindling to a point and vanishing. And on every side, too, Drake heard the quick beat of horses, and the rattle of wheels struck out not from silence, but from a dull eternal hum like the hum of a mill, sharp particular notes emerging incessantly from a monotonous volume of sound.

It was just this aspect and this noise of restless activity which had always appealed to Drake, and had satisfied him with an assurance that he was on the road to the fulfilment of his aims. He had achieved something of his desires, however small. He was in London working at certain schemes of which he did not doubt the ultimate success. They were built upon a foundation of knowledge arduously gained and tested. The rising in Matanga, if it took place, might delay success, but success would surely come. He might then look forward with confidence to a seat in that Parliament on which the light was burning, to a share perhaps finally in its executive.

But to-night he found that there was something wanting in the contemplation of these aims, something wanting in the very outlook from his window. He needed Clarice here in his balcony by his side, and he pictured the shine of her eyes bent towards him in the dark. And the perception of that need held him in check, gave him a hint of warning that the thought of her might become as a wedge driven into the framework of his purposes and splitting them.

He could still draw back, he assured himself. But if he went on and won! He felt the blood surging through his veins. He might win; there was just a chance. The Gorley incident had made no real difference in Clarice's friendliness. When once, indeed, she had grown used to it, she had seemed almost to express some queer sort of sympathy with him.

Drake closed the window and sat down to calculate the time at which he would be sufficiently established to make known his suit. He fixed that time definitely in July. July! The name sounded pleasantly with its ripple of liquid syllables. Drake found himself repeating it when he should have been at work. It began to rise to his lips the moment a date was asked of him, as the only date at all worth mentioning. Fielding came down to Drake's office in Old Broad Street, in order to apply for shares in 'Matanga Concessions.'

'You had better wait,' said Drake. 'I will let you know before they are offered to the public.'

'That will be soon?'

'Not for the moment. There's the possibility of this rising. Let the country quiet down first!'

'But when do you propose?'

'July.'

'July? That's a long time to come.'

Drake coloured to the roots of his hair. 'I beg your pardon,' he said with evident embarrassment; 'much sooner than that of course. I was thinking of some one else.' He made matters worse by a hurried correction of 'some one' to 'something.'

Fielding noticed the embarrassment and the correction, and drew conclusions. They were conclusions, he thought, of which Mrs. Willoughby should be advised, and he drove to her house accordingly. He had ceased to feel displeasure at Mrs. Willoughby's conduct, for since he had studiously refrained from betraying the slightest irritation at Mallinson's visits, those visits had amazingly diminished.

'Did he happen to mention the date of the month and the time of the day?' was Mrs. Willoughby's comment.

'It sounds cold-blooded? Hardly, if you knew the man. He looks on life as a sort of draughtboard. So many definite moves to be made forward upon definite lines. Then you're crowned king and can move as you please, backwards if you like, till the end of the game.'

'He will be crowned king in July?'

'So I imagine.'

Meanwhile Drake worked on through March and April,

A. E. W. Mason

outwardly untroubled, but inwardly asking himself ever: 'Shall I win? Shall I win?' The question besieged him. Patient he could be, none more so, when the end in view was to be gained by present even though gradual endeavour; but this passive waiting was a lid shut down on him, forcing his energies inwards to prey upon himself. His impatience, moreover, was increased by the increasing prospects of his undertaking. Additional reports had been received from his engineer appraising at a still higher value the quality of the land. He spoke too of a tract of country bordering Drake's concession on the north, and advised application for it. Biedermann, besides, had taken up the project warmly. The company was to come out early in May; there would be few shares open to the public, and the revolution had not taken place.

Why should he wait till July after all? Drake felt inclined to argue the question one Sunday afternoon in London's lilac time, as he walked across the green park towards Beaufort Gardens. He found Miss Le Mesurier alone and in a melancholy mood. She was singing weariful ballads in an undertone as he entered the room, and she rose dispiritedly to welcome him.

'It's seldom one finds you alone,' he said, and his face showed his satisfaction.

'I don't know,' she replied. 'It seems to me sometimes that I am always alone, even when people are by,' and her eyelids drooped.

'You?'

Clarice's sincerity was of the artist's sort implying a subconsciousness of an audience. She recognised from the accent upon the *you*, that her little speech had not failed of its effect. She continued more cheerfully: 'Aunt has gone up to Highgate to see some relations, and papa's asleep in the library.'

'You were singing. I hope you won't stop.'

'I was only passing the time.'

'You will make me think I intrude.'

'I'll prove to you that you don't,' and she went back to the piano. Drake seated himself at the side of it, facing her and facing the open window. The window-ledges were ablaze with flowers, and the scent of them poured into the room on a flood of sunshine.

Clarice was moved by a sudden whim to a change of humour. She sprang from her dejection to the extreme of good spirits. Her singing proved it, for she chose a couple of light-hearted French ballads, and sang them with a dainty humour which matched the daintiness of the words and music. Her shrugs and pouts, the pretty arching of her eyebrows, the whimsical note of mockery in her voice, represented her to Drake under a new aspect, helped to complete her in his thoughts much as her voice, very sweet and clear for all its small compass, completed in some queer way the flowers and sunshine. Her manner, however, did more than that; it gave to him, conscious of a certain stiffness and inflexibility of temperament, an inner sense of completion anticipated from his hope of a time when their lives would join. He leaned forward in his chair, watching the play of her face, the lights and shadows in the curls of her hair, the nimble touch of her fingers on the keys. Clarice stopped suddenly. 'You don't sing?'

'I have no accomplishments at all.'

She laughed and began to play one of Chopin's nocturnes. Her fingers rattled against the ivory on a run up the piano. She stopped and took a ring from her right hand; Drake noticed that it was the emerald ring which he had seen winking in the firelight on that evening when she had covered her face from him. She dropped the ring on the top of the piano at Drake's side. It spun round once or twice, and then settled down with a little tinkling whirr upon the rim of its hoop Drake fancied that the removal of this particular ring was in some inexplicable way of hopeful augury to him.

Clarice resumed her playing, but as she neared the end of the nocturne, Drake perceived that there was a growing change, a declension, in her style. She seemed to lose the spirit of the nocturne and even her command on the instrument; the firm touch faltered into indecision, from indecision to absolute unsteadiness; the notes, before clear and distinct, now slurred into one another with a tremulous wavering.

'You are fond of music?' she asked at length, with something of an effort.

'Very,' he replied, 'though it puzzles me. It's like opening a book written in a language you don't understand. You get a glimpse of a meaning here and there, but no meaning really. I can't explain what I feel,' he added, with a laugh. 'I want Mallinson to help me.'

'You admire Mr. Mallinson?' asked Clarice, stopping suddenly.

'Well, one always admires the class of work one can't do oneself, eh?'

'That's very generous of you.'

'Why generous?' Drake leaned suddenly forward. His habit

of putting questions abrupt and straight to the point had discomposed Miss Le Mesurier upon an occasion before. She answered hurriedly. 'I mean—you spoke as if you meant that class of work was above your own.'

'Oh, there's no basis of comparison.'

Clarice seized the opportunity, and inquired after the prospects of his work in Matanga.

'The place should do,' said Drake. 'The land's good, there's a river running through, and I have got picked men to settle on it; all English, that's the point. But you said generous. I don't see.'

Clarice switched him on the subject of English colonisation. 'It's necessary to have Englishmen to start it? Why?'

'Oh, well,' said Drake. 'It's easy enough to see, if you can compare English with the foreign colonies.' He rose from his chair and launched forth, walking about the room. 'Look at the Germans! There are seven hundred German colonists, all told, in the German colonies, and each of them costs the German tax-payer little short of eight hundred a year. How many of them are in the English colonies? And what's the reason? Why, they want to have the institutions of the Fatherland ready-made in five minutes. They need the colonies made before they can prosper in it. The French are better, but they are spoilt by officialdom. The Englishman just adapts himself to the conditions, and sets to work to adapt the conditions to himself too. He strikes a sort of mean, and the Home Government leaves him alone—leaves him too much alone some say, and rightly, in cases. There's a distinction to be drawn, and it's difficult to draw it so far away. It's this, when the colony's made, then it isn't a bad thing for the Government to keep a fairly tight hold on it. But in the making it's best left to itself; you can lay a cable between London and a colony too soon for the good of that colony. There's no fear of the colonist forgetting the mother country—he may forget the Home Government, does at times, and then there's a mistake or two. But that's the defect of the quality.' He checked himself abruptly. 'But I'm running away from what we were talking about. Yes; I think we shall do all right in Matanga.'

'You don't mean to go back there yourself?'

'Not to live there. To tell the truth, I think there's a man or two wanted in England just now, who has had a practical experience of our colonies.' Drake spoke without the least trace of boastfulness, but in a tone of quiet self-reliance, and Clarice had a thrill of intuition that he would not have said so much as that to any one but herself.

Clarice began to play again, this time a waltz tune. Drake came over to the piano, and stood leaning upon the lid of it; he took up the ring and turned it over in his fingers. She said thoughtfully:

'I suppose that's true of men as well'; and then, with a hesitating correction, 'I mean of men like you.'

'What's true?'

'Well, that they are best without—help from any one—that they stand in no need of it.' She spoke quite seriously, with a note almost of regret.

'Oh, I don't know that,' he answered, with a laugh. 'It would be a rash thing to say. Of course a man ought to depend upon himself.'

'Oh, of course,' she agreed, and went on playing.

Drake was still holding the ring, and he said slowly:

'You remember that afternoon I told you about'—he hesitated for a second—'Gorley?' Clarice looked up in surprise.

'Yes,' she said.

'You were wearing this ring. You hid your face in your hands. It was the last thing I saw of you.'

She lowered her eyes from his face, and said, with a certain timidity, 'He gave it to me.'

Drake started and leaned on the piano.

'And you still wear it?' he asked sharply.

She nodded, but without looking at him. Drake rose upright, straightening himself; for a moment or two he stood looking at her, and then he walked away towards the window. His hat was lying on a table close by it.

'But I don't think that I shall again,' she murmured. She heard him turn quickly round and come back. He stood behind her; she could see his shadow thrown across the bar of sunlight on the carpet; but he did not speak. Clarice became anxious that he should, and yet afraid too. The music began to falter again; once she stopped completely, and let her fingers rest upon the keys, as though she had no power to lift them and continue. Then she struck a chord with a loud defiance. If only he would move, she thought—if only he would come round and stand in front of her! It would be so much easier to speak, to divert him. So long as he stood silent and motionless behind her, she felt, in a strange manner, at his mercy.

She rose from her seat suddenly, and confronted him. There was challenge in the movement, but none the less her eyes sought the ground, and, once face to face with him, she stood in an attitude of submission.

'What does that mean?' she heard him ask in a low voice. 'You won't wear it again.'

She did not answer, but in spite of herself, against her will, she raised her eyes until they met his. She heard a cry, hoarse and passionate; she felt herself lifted, caught, and held against him. She saw his eyes above hers, burning into hers; she felt the pressure of two lips upon hers, and her own respond obediently.

'Is it true?' The words were whispered into her ear with an accent of wonder, almost of awe.

'Yes,' she whispered back, compelled to the answer, subservient to his touch, to his words, and, to the full, conscious of her subservience. She felt the big breath he drew in answering her monosyllable. He held her unresisting, passive in his arms, watching her cheeks fire. She realised, in a kind of detached way, that he was holding her so that the tips of her toes only touched the floor, and somehow that seemed of a piece with the rest. Then he set her down, and stood apart, keeping her hands. 'It's funny,' he said, 'how one goes on year after year, quite satisfied, knowing nothing of this, meaning not to know.'

She caught at the phrase and stammered, 'Perhaps that was wise.'

'It was. For so I met you.'

He released her hands, and she sank into the nearest chair.

Drake walked to the window and stood facing the sunlight, breathing it in. 'Clarice,' she heard him murmur, with a shake of his shoulders like a great Newfoundland dog; and then the cry of a newspaper boy shouting the headlines of a special edition rasped into the room.

Drake leaned out of the window. 'Hi!' he called, and tossed a penny into the street.

'Threepence,' shouted the boy from below.

'It's a penny paper,' cried Drake.

'Threepence. There's a corner in 'em.'

Clarice listened to the argument. Most men, she thought helplessly, don't buy newspapers the moment they have been accepted, and, at all events, it is an occasion when they are disposed to throw their money about. It made no difference of any kind to him.

Drake finally got the better of the bargain, and the paper was brought up to the room. Clarice saw Drake open it hurriedly, and his face cloud and harden as he glanced down the column.

'What's the matter?' she asked in a rising voice.

'A rebellion in Matanga,' he said slowly. 'I thought that danger was averted,' and there was a distinct note of self-reproach in his tone.

Clarice felt her heart beat quicker. She rose from her chair. 'What does that mean to you?' she asked.

'Delay,' he replied, with the self-reproach yet more

accentuated. 'Nothing more, I am sure; but it does mean that.'

'Nothing more?'

He noticed an expression of disappointment upon the girl's face, and, mistaking it, repeated, 'Nothing more than that, Clarice.' He took a step towards her. 'Of course I ought not to have spoken to you yet,—not until everything was settled. I am sorry—of course it will come out all right, only till then it wasn't fair. I didn't mean to,—not even when I came this afternoon. But seeing you,—I wasn't strong enough,—I gave in.'

Clarice felt a pulse of satisfaction, and her lips shaped to a smile.

'Ah, you don't regret it,' he exclaimed, and the look of humiliation passed from his face. 'Your father's in the library,' he went on; 'I had better go and tell him. Shall I go alone, or will you come with me?'

'No, you go; I will wait here.'

She stood alone in the centre of the room while Drake went downstairs, staring fixedly in front of her. Once or twice she set her hands to her forehead and drew them down her flushed cheeks. Then she walked to the window. There was something floating on the edge of her mind, just eluding her. A thought was it, or a phrase? If a phrase, who had spoken it? She began to remember; it was something Stephen Drake had said, but about what? And then, in a flash, her recollection defined it for her. It was about moonlight being absorbed into the darkness of an African veld, just soaking into it like water into dry ground. She had a vision of the wide rolling plain, black from sky's rim to sky's rim, and the moonlight pouring a futile splendour into its lap. She moved with a quick and almost desperate run to the door, opened it, and leaned over the balustrade of the staircase. The hall was empty and no sound of voices came from the library. She stepped cautiously down the stairs; as she reached the last step the door of the library opened and Drake appeared on the threshold.

Clarice leaned against the wall, holding her hand to her heart.

'Why, Clarice!' he cried, and started towards her.

'Hush!' She tried to whisper the word, but her voice rose. She thrust out a hand between herself and Drake, and cast a startled glance across his shoulder, expecting to see her father come forward smiling congratulations at her. Drake caught the outstretched hand, and, setting an arm about her waist, drew her into the library.

'I have not seen Mr. Le Mesurier,' he said; 'he's out, I am afraid.'

The room was empty. Clarice looked round it, doubting her eyes, and with a sudden revulsion of feeling dropped into a chair by the table and sat with her face buried in her arms in a flood of tears.

A. E. W. Mason

CHAPTER X

Drake bent over her, stroking her hair with a gentle helpless movement of his hand and occasionally varying his consolation by a pat on the shoulders. The puffed sleeves of silk yielding under his touch gave him a queer impression of the girl's fragility.

'Oh don't, child!' he entreated. 'It's my fault for speaking so soon. But really there's nothing to fear—nothing. It'll all come out right—not a doubt of that. You'll see.'

Consolation of this kind did but make the tears flow yet more freely. Drake perceived the fact and stood aside, wondering perplexedly at the reason. The sound of each sob jerked at his heart; he began to walk restlessly about the room. The storm, from its very violence, however, wore itself quickly out; the sobs became less convulsive, less frequent. Clarice raised her head from her arms and stared out of the window opposite, with just now and then a little shiver and heave of her back.

Drake stopped his walk and advanced to her. She anticipated his speech, turning with a start to face him.

'You haven't seen my father?'

'No; the servant told me he had gone out. But I wrote a note saying I would call again this evening. It is under your elbow.'

Clarice picked up the crumpled envelope and looked at it absently.

'Stephen,' she said, and she tripped upon the name, 'there's something I ought to tell you—now. But it's rather difficult.'

Drake walked to the window and stood with his back towards her. She felt grateful to him for the action, and was a little surprised at the tact which had prompted it.

'Yes?' he said.

'We are not very well off,' she continued; 'perhaps you know that.'

'Yes,' he interrupted.

'But the position's more complicated than you can know'; she was speaking carefully, weighing her words. 'Of course you know that I have a sister younger than myself. She's at school in Brussels. Well, by the Sark laws, the Seigneurie can't be split up between the members of a family. I think it's the same with all land there. It must go—what's the word?—unencumbered to the eldest child. So it must come to me—all of it. That leaves my sister still to be provided for. Father explained the whole thing to me. As it is, he has as much as he can do to keep the Seigneurie up. This house we can't really afford, but father thought he ought to take it,—well, for my sake, I suppose. So, you see, whatever money he has he must leave to my sister, and there's still the Seigneurie for me to keep up.'

'Yes, I understand. You are bound by duty, if you marry, to marry some one with means. But, Clarice, it won't be long to wait,' and he turned back from the window into the room.

'But till then—don't you see? Of course I know you will be successful,' and she laid considerable emphasis on the *I*.

Drake reflected for a moment. 'You mean there would be trouble between your father and you. The weight of it would fall on you. He might distrust me. Yes; after all, why should he not? But still the thing's done, isn't it?'

Clarice rose from her chair and walked to the grate. A fire was burning, and she still held Drake's letter in her hand. 'We might keep it to ourselves,' she said diffidently. She saw Drake's forehead contract. 'For my sake,' she said softly, laying a hand upon his sleeve. She lifted a tear-stained face up to his with the prettiest appeal. 'I know you hate it, but it will spare me so much.'

He said nothing, and she dropped the letter into the fire.

As Drake was leaving the house she heard, through the closed door, the sound of her father's voice in the hall speaking to him, and felt a momentary pang of alarm. The next instant, however, she laughed. He might have broken his word to himself; he would not break it to her.

Drake went home, reckoning up the harm he had done with a feeling of degradation quite new to him. Not the least part of that harm was the compromise finally agreed upon. But for the traces of tears upon the girl's cheeks, he would hardly have agreed to it even in the face of her appeal. Once alone, however, he saw clearly all—the deception that it implied—deception which involved the girl, too, as well as himself. He rose the next day in no more equable frame of mind, and leaving his office at three o'clock in the afternoon, walked along Cheapside, Holborn, and Oxford Street, and turned down Bond Street, meaning to pass an hour in the fencing-rooms half-way down St. James Street. At the corner of Bruton Street he came face to face with Miss Le Mesurier. She coloured for an instant, and then came frankly forward and held out her hand.

'It's funny meeting you here,' she said, and laughed without the least embarrassment.

Drake turned and walked by her side with a puzzled conjecture at the reason of woman's recuperative powers. Clarice's eyes were as clear, her forehead as sunny, as though she had clean wiped yesterday from her consciousness. The conjecture, however, brought the reality of yesterday only yet more home to him. He stopped in the street and said abruptly, 'Clarice, I can't.'

She stopped in her turn and drew a little pattern on the pavement with the point of her umbrella. 'Why?'

A passer-by jostled Drake in the back. Standing there they were blocking the way. 'Isn't there anywhere we could go? Tea? One drinks tea at this hour, eh?'

'No.'

Clarice felt more mistress of herself in the open street, more able to cope with Drake while they walked in a throng. She remembered enough of yesterday to avoid even the makeshift solitude of a tea-table in a public room. 'Let us walk on,' she said. 'Can't you explain as we go? I am late.'

She moved forward as she spoke, and Drake kept pace with her, shortening his strides. The need of doing that, trifle though it was, increased his sense of responsibility towards her. 'It's so abominably deceitful, and it's my doing. I should involve you in the deceit.'

Clarice glanced at him sharply. The distress of his voice was repeated in the expression of her face. There was no doubting that he spoke sincerely.

'I had better see your father to—day,' he added.

'No,' she replied energetically; and, after a moment's pause, 'There's another way.'

'Well?'

'Let everything be as it was before yesterday. I shall not change. It will be better for you to be free. Come to me when you are ready.'

She signed to a passing hansom, and it drew up by the curb. She got into it while Drake stood with brows knitted, revolving the proposal in his mind. 'But you see it can't be the same,' he said; 'because I kissed you, didn't I?'

'Yes, you did,' she replied.

The tremble of laughter in her voice made him look up to her face. The rose deepened in her cheeks, and the laughter rippled out. 'You are quaint,' she said. 'I will forget—well—what you said, until you are ready. Till then it's to be just as it was before—only not less. You are not to stay away'; and without waiting for an answer she lifted the trap, gave the cabman his order, and drove off. Drake watched the hansom disappear, and absently retraced his steps down the street. He stopped once or twice and stared vaguely into the shop-windows. One of these was a jeweller's, and he turned sharply away from it and quickened his pace towards the fencing-rooms. How could it be the same, he asked himself, when the mere sparkle of an emerald ring in a jeweller's shop-window aroused in him a feeling of distaste?

Towards the end of this week Clarice called upon Mrs. Willoughby, and seemed for the moment put out on finding that Mallinson and Fielding were present. Mrs. Willoughby welcomed her all the more warmly because she was finding it difficult to keep the peace between her two visitors. She understood Clarice's embarrassment when Percy Conway arrived close upon her heels. Clarice, however, quietly handed him over to Mrs. Willoughby, and seated herself beside Mallinson in one of the windows. 'I see nothing of you now,' she said, and she looked the reproach of the hardly-used. 'I thought we had agreed to be friends?'

Mallinson sighed wearily. 'I will come and call—some day,' he said dejectedly.

'I have not so many friends that I can afford a loss,' she answered pathetically; and then, 'Tell me about yourself. What are you doing?'

'Nothing.'

'No work?'

'No.' Mallinson shook his head.

'Why?'

'I have no incentive—nothing to work for.'

'That's cruel.'

They played out their farce of sham sentiment with a luxurious earnestness for a little while longer, and then Mallinson went away.

'So he's doing no work?' said Fielding maliciously to Miss Le Mesurier. He leaned forward as he spoke from the embrasure of the second window, which was in a line with, and but a few feet apart from, that at which she was sitting.

Miss Le Mesurier flushed, and asked, 'How did you hear?'

'Both windows are open. Mallinson was leaning out.'

The girl's confusion increased, and with it Fielding's enjoyment. He repeated, 'So he's doing no work?'

'A thousand a year, don't you know?' said Conway, with a sneer. 'It would make a man like that lazy.'

'It's not laziness,' exclaimed Clarice indignantly. She was filled with pity for Mallinson, and experienced, too, a sort of reflex pity for herself as the inappropriate instrument of his suffering. She was consequently altogether tuned to tenderness for him. 'It's not laziness at all. It's— it's—' She cast about for a laudatory explanation.

'Well, what?' Fielding pressed genially.

'It's the artistic temperament,' she exclaimed triumphantly.

Fielding laughed at her vindication, and Miss Le Mesurier walked across the room and said good-bye to Mrs. Willoughby. Conway rose at the same time, and the pair left the house together.

'What a liar that man is!' said Fielding.

'What man?' asked Mrs. Willoughby.

'Why, Mallinson. He said he was doing no work because he had no incentive. As a matter of fact, I happen to know that he is working rather hard.'

'What did Clarice say?'

'What you might expect. She melted into sympathy.'

Mrs. Willoughby looked puzzled. 'Yet she went off with Percy Conway immediately afterwards,' she said, and then laughed at her recollections of a previous visit from that gentleman.

'Yes; and absolutely unconscious of the humour of her behaviour,' said Fielding. 'That's so delightful about her.' He paused for a second and asked, 'Have you ever been inside a camera obscura? You get a picture, an impression, very vivid, very accurate, of something that is actually happening. Then some one pulls a string and you get a totally different picture, equally vivid, equally accurate, of something else which is actually happening. There is no trace of the first picture in the second. Then they open a shutter and you see nothing but a plain white slab. Somehow I always think of Miss Le Mesurier's mind.'

After leaving Mrs. Willoughby's, Conway and Miss Le Mesurier walked together in the direction of Beaufort Gardens.

'Do you see much of Mr. Drake?' she asked, after a considerable silence.

'Not as much as one would wish to. He's generally busy.'

'You like him, then?' she asked curiously. 'Why?'

'Don't you? There's an absence of pretension about him. Nothing of the born-to-command air, but insensibly you find yourself believing in him, following him. I believe even Fielding finds that as well. When Drake first came back I used to stand up for him—well, because, perhaps, I had a reason of my own. I am not sure that I believed all I said, but I am sure now I should say exactly the same and believe every word of it.'

He spoke with a quiet conviction which gave solid weight to his words, owing to its contrast with the flighty enthusiasm which was the usual characteristic of his eulogies.

'You mentioned Mr. Fielding,' she said.

'Yes; haven't you heard? He's investing in Matanga Concessions, and largely for him. He's often seen in Drake's office.'

Clarice walked along in silence for some way further. Then she said, with a distinct irritation in her voice, 'I suppose it all comes from the fact that Mr. Drake doesn't seem to need any one to rely upon, or—well—any particular incentive to work.'

Conway glanced at Miss Le Mesurier with a slight surprise. She was generally given to accept facts without inquiry into their causes. 'I shouldn't wonder if you are right. Drake, I should think, would find his incentive in the work itself. Yes; I believe you *are* right. It's just his single-mindedness which influences one. There are certain ideas fixed in his mind, combined into one aim, and he lets nothing interfere to obscure that aim.'

So he spoke; so, too, Clarice believed, and that picture of moonlight on the veld became yet more vivid, yet more frequent in her thoughts. Pondering upon it, her fancy led her to exaggerate Drake into the likeness of some Egyptian god, that sits with huge hands resting upon massive knees, and works out its own schemes behind indifferent eyes. The sight of him, and the sound of commonplace words from his mouth, would at times make her laugh at the conception and restore her to her former familiarity with him. But the fancy returned to her, and, each time, added a fresh layer to the colour of her thoughts. She came now and again to betray a positive shrinking from him. Drake noticed it; he noticed something else as well: in the first week of July the emerald ring reappeared upon her finger.

In the second week Mr. Le Mesurier removed his household gods to Sark. It was his habit to spend the summer months upon the island, and to entertain there his friends in succession. He invited both Mrs. Willoughby and Stephen Drake. The former accepted, the latter, being on the eve of floating the Matanga Concessions, declined for the present to Clarice's great relief, but promised to come later. The company was floated towards the end of the month, and with immediate success. Mr. Le Mesurier read out at breakfast a letter which he had received from Drake, announcing that every share had been taken up on the very day of flotation.

'Then he is coming,' said Clarice. 'When?'

Mr. Le Mesurier mistook his daughter's anxiety, and smiled satisfaction at her. 'To-morrow,' he replied; 'but only for three days at first. There's some new development he speaks of. He will have to leave again on Saturday for a fortnight.'

Clarice sat thoughtfully for a minute or two. Then she asked: 'Did you invite Mr. Mallinson this summer?'

Mr. Le Mesurier shuffled his feet under the table. 'No, my dear,' he said. 'I forgot all about it; and now I don't see that we shall have room.'

'Oh yes,' replied Clarice quickly. 'He might have Mr. Drake's room during that fortnight. I think we ought to ask him. We always have, and it will look rather strange if we leave him out this summer. I will get aunt to write after breakfast.'

Mr. Le Mesurier glanced at Mrs. Willoughby, but made no active resistance, and Clarice took care that the letter was despatched by that day's post. On the next day she organised a picnic in Little Sark, and returned to the Seigneurie at an hour which gave her sufficient time to dress for dinner, but no margin for welcoming visitors. In consequence she only saw Drake at the dinner-table. She saw little of him afterwards, for Mr. Le Mesurier pounced upon him after dinner. 'I want to introduce you to Burl,' he said. 'He's Parliamentary agent for the Northern Counties. There's a constituency in Yorkshire where my brother lives, and I rather think Burl wants a candidate.'

Drake was presented to a gentleman six feet three in his socks, deep-chested, broad-shouldered, with a square rugged face on the slant from the forehead to the chin. Mrs. Willoughby said he looked like a pirate, and rumour made of her simile a fact. It was known that, late one night in the smoking-room of the Seigneurie, he had owned to silver-running on the coast of Mexico. Mr. Burl and Drake passed most of that evening smoking together in the garden. Similarly on the next day Clarice avoided a private interview with Drake. On the other hand, however, he made no visible effort to secure one. Mrs. Willoughby wondered at his reticence, and did more than wonder. She had by this time espoused his cause, and knowing no half-measures in her enthusiasms, saw his chances slipping from him, with considerable irritation. She was consequently provoked to hint her advice to him on the evening before he was to leave.

Drake shook his head and replied frankly: 'One can be too previous. I made that mistake once before, and I don't mean to repeat it.'

He remained silent for a moment or two, and added: 'I think I'll tell you about it, Mrs. Willoughby. You have guessed some part of the story, and you are Clarice's friend, and mine too, I believe.'

With an impulsiveness rare in him, which however served to rivet him yet more firmly in Mrs. Willoughby's esteem, he confided to her the history of his proposal and its lame result. 'So you see,' he concluded, 'I am not likely to risk a repetition of the incident.'

'But,' said she, 'surely there's no risk now?'

'Very likely, but there is just a little. This next fortnight will, I think, make everything secure, but I must wait that fortnight.'

'Well, I believe you are unwise.' Drake turned to her quickly. 'Why?'

'Mr. Mallinson takes your place for the fortnight. Of course I don't know. Clarice has given up confiding in me. But I really think you are unwise.'

Drake sat staring in front of him. He was considering Mallinson's visit in conjunction with the reappearance of the emerald ring upon Miss Le Mesurier's finger. 'All the same,' he said at length, 'I shall wait.'

The reason for this hesitation he explained more fully to Clarice herself some half an hour afterwards. He found her standing by herself upon the terrace. She started nervously as he approached, and it seemed to him that her whole figure stiffened to a posture of defence. She said nothing, however, and for a while they stood side by side looking seawards across the breadth of the island. The ground stretched away broken into little hollows and little hills,—downs in vignette. A cheery yellow light streamed from the windows of a cottage in a dip of the grass; the slates of a roof glistened from a group of sycamores like a mirror in a dark frame; the whole island lay bared to the moonlight. Towards the edge of it the land rose upwards to a ridge, but there was a cleft in the ridge opposite to where they stood, and through the cleft they looked downwards to the sea.

Clarice spoke of the moonbeams broken into sparkles by the ripple of the water.

'Like a shoal of silver coins,' said Drake.

'Wouldn't you like to hear them clink?' she asked petulantly.

Then he said: 'Miss Le Mesurier'—and the change in his voice made the girl turn swiftly to face him—'I leave Sark to-morrow morning by the early boat, so I thought I would say good-bye to you to-night.'

'But you are coming back,' she said quickly; 'I shall see you, of course, when you come back. What takes you away?'

'There's some land in Matanga which bounds my concession on the north, and I want to get hold of it. It's, I believe, quite as good, and may be better, than mine, and I know that some people are after it. It wouldn't help me if another company was to be started; and as the President of the Matanga

Republic is on his way to England, I thought that I had better go out to Madeira, catch his steamer there, and secure a concession of it before he reaches England.'

Clarice gave a laugh. 'Then we are to expect you in a fortnight?'

'Yes, in a fortnight,' and he laid a significance upon the word which Clarice did not mistake. It was spoken with an accent of entreaty.

But indeed she needed no emphasis to fix it in her mind. The word besieged her; she caught herself uttering it, and while she uttered it the time itself seemed to have slipped by. She had but to say 'No' at the end of the fortnight, she assured herself, and she knew that she would only have to say it once. But the memory of that Sunday afternoon in Beaufort Gardens lay upon her like a load crushing all the comfort out of her knowledge.

Drake caught his steamer at Southampton, and the President at Madeira. He was received warmly as an old acquaintance, warily as a negotiator. However, he extracted the concession as the boat passed up Southampton Water, and disembarked with a signed memorandum in his pocket. At Southampton post-office he received a bundle of letters which had been forwarded to him from his chambers in London. He slipped them into his coat, and went at once on board the Guernsey steamer. At Guernsey, the next morning, he embarked on the little boat which runs between Guernsey and Sark. The sun was a golden fire upon the water; the race of the tides no more than a ripple. The island stuck out its great knees into the sea and lolled in the heat. Half-way across Drake bethought him of the letters. He took them out and glanced over the envelopes. One was in Clarice's handwriting. It announced to him her engagement with Sidney Mallinson.

CHAPTER XI

Of Drake's arrival at the Seigneurie Mrs. Willoughby wrote some account to Hugh Fielding, who was taking the waters for no ailment whatever at Marienbad. 'I was surprised to see him,' she wrote, 'because Clarice told me that she had written to him. Clarice was running down the stairs when he came into the hall. She stopped suddenly as she caught sight of him, clutched at the balustrade, slipped a heel upon the edge of the step, and with a cry pitched straight into his arms at the bottom. Mr. Mallinson came out of the library while he was holding her. Clarice was not hurt, however, and Mr. Drake set her down. "I didn't pass through London," he said, and he seemed to be apologising. "My letters were forwarded to Southampton, and I only opened them on the Sark steamer." Then he congratulated them both. I spoke to Mr. Drake the same evening on the terrace here, foolishly hinting the feminine consolation that he was well free from a girl of Clarice's fickleness. He was in arms on the instant. One gets at truth only by experiment, and through repeated mistakes. Why except women's hearts from the same law? I give his opinion, not his words. He doesn't talk of "women's hearts." You know his trick of suggesting when it comes to talk of the feelings. I slid into a worse blunder and sympathised with him. He replied that it didn't make the difference to him which I might think. I felt as if a stream of ice-water had been turned down my back on Christmas Day. However, he went on in a sort of shame-faced style, like a schoolboy caught talking sentiment. "One owes her a debt for having cared for her, and the debt remains." He stayed out his visit and left this morning. He goes to Switzerland, and asked for your address. His is *The Bear, Grindelwald.* Write to him there; better, join him. He talks of going out to Matanga later in the year for a few months. So there's the end of the business, or rather one hopes so. I used to hope that Clarice would wake up some morning into a real woman and find herself—isn't that the phrase? I hope the reverse now; that she and her husband will philander along to the close of the chapter. But I prefer your word,—to the close of the "comedy," say. It implies something artificial. Mallinson and Clarice give me that impression,—as of Watteau figures mincing a gavotte, and made more unreal by the juxtaposition of a man. Let's hope they will never perceive the flimsiness of their pretty bows and ribbons! But I think of your one o'clock in the morning of the masquerade ball, and frankly I am afraid. I look at the three without—well, with as little prejudice as weak woman may. Mallinson, you know him—always on the artist's see-saw between exaltation and despair. Doesn't that make for shiftiness generally? Clarice I don't understand; but I incline to your idea of her as at the mercy of every momentary emotion, and the more for what has happened this week. Since her engagement she seems to have lost her fear of Stephen Drake. She has been all unexpressed sympathy. And Drake? There's the danger, I am sure—a danger not of the usual kind. Had he been unscrupulous he might have ridden roughshod over Clarice long before now. But he's too scrupulous for that. I think that he misses greatness as we understand it, through excess of scruple. But there's that saying of his about a debt incurred to Clarice by the man caring for her. Well, convince him that he can pay it by any sacrifice; won't he pay it? Convince him that it would benefit her if he lay in the mud; wouldn't he do it? I don't know. I made a little prayer yesterday night,

A. E. W. Mason

grotesque enough, but very sincere, that there might be no fifth act of tragedy to make a discord of your comedy.'

Fielding received Mrs. Willoughby's command to join Drake with a grin at her conception of him as fit company for a gentleman disappointed in his love-affairs. He nevertheless obeyed it, and travelling to Grindelwald found Drake waiting him on the platform with the hands of an oakum-picker, and a face toned uniformly to the colour of a ripe pippin. 'You have been climbing mountains, I suppose?' asked Fielding.

'Yes,' nodded Drake.

'Well, don't ask me to join you. It produces a style of conversation I don't like.'

Drake laughed, and protested that nothing was further from his intention. Certain letters, however, which Fielding wrote to Mrs. Willoughby during this period proved that he did join him, and more than once. The two men returned to London half-way through September.

On the journey from Dover to Charing Cross Drake asked whether Mrs. Willoughby was in town. He was informed that at the moment she was visiting in Scotland, but she was expected to pass through London at the end of a fortnight. Drake wrote a note to her address asking her to spare him a few moments when she came south, and receiving a cordial assent with the statement of the most favourable hour, walked across one evening to Knightsbridge. Mrs. Willoughby remarked a certain constraint in his manner, and awaited tentacle questions concerning Sidney Mallinson and Clarice. She said: 'You look well. You have enjoyed your holiday.'

'I had an amusing companion.'

'You have given him some spark of your activity,' and the sentence was pitched to convey thanks.

'Then you have seen him?' Drake's embarrassment became more pronounced. He paused for a second and then rose and walked across the room. 'You know, I suppose,' he resumed, 'that I am going out to Matanga in a month.'

'I heard something of that from Mr. Fielding,' she said gently.

'Yes,' he said, with a change in his voice to brisk cheerfulness. 'It seemed to me that I ought to go. Our interests there are rather large now. I consulted my fellow-directors, and they agreed with me.'

The sudden disappearance of the constraint which had marked him surprised Mrs. Willoughby. 'But can you leave London?' she asked.

'Oh yes; I have made arrangements for that,' he replied. 'I have got Burl to look after things here.'

'Mr. Burl?'

'Yes; it's rather funny,' said Drake, with a laugh. 'He came to ask me whether I was disposed to take up politics. There was a constituency in Yorkshire he could arrange for me to stand for—Bentbridge. Do you know it?'

'I have been there. Mr. Le Mesurier has a brother just outside the town. It was there, I believe, that he became acquainted with Mr. Burl.'

'So I gathered. Well, I wanted the question left open for a bit. Then Burl made another proposal. He said they wanted a paper in the district. There were some people ready to back the idea, but they didn't have quite enough capital. Burl wanted me to provide the rest. He didn't get it, but he nearly did, and it struck me that he was just the man I wanted. So after he had had his say, I had mine, and he has thrown up politics and joined me.' Drake ended his story with a laugh, and added, 'I think I am lucky to have got hold of him.'

'Then you don't mean to go away for good?' exclaimed Mrs. Willoughby.

'Oh dear no! What on earth made you think that? But I will be away a year, I think,—and—and, that's just the point.' His embarrassment returned as suddenly as it had left him.

'I don't understand.'

'Well, I had an idea of persuading Fielding to go with me.' He blurted the proposal brusquely. 'He's interested, you see, in the success of the colony, and—well, altogether, I didn't think it would be a bad thing.'

Mrs. Willoughby walked to the window and looked out of it for a few seconds. 'What does Mr. Fielding say?' she asked.

'I haven't broached the subject to him yet. I thought I wouldn't before—' He stopped and made no effort to finish the sentence.

'It's a year,' she said slowly, lengthening out the word. 'Yes, only a year,' said he briskly, and Mrs. Willoughby smiled in spite of herself. She thought of the new air of alertness which Fielding had worn since his return from Switzerland. She came back to Drake and held out her hand to him. 'You think very wisely for your friends,' she said.

'It's an inspiriting business to see a community in the making,' he answered; 'especially when there's money to help it to make itself quickly.'

He wished her good-bye and moved to the door. As he opened it he said, 'By the way, is the date of the marriage fixed?' but without turning towards her.

She said, 'Yes, the 8th of December,' and she saw his shoulders brace, and the weight of his body come backwards from the ball of the foot on to the heel.

'Ah! I shall be in Africa by then,' he said.

It was in fact near upon the end of February that the river-steamer plying between the settlement and the coast of Matanga brought to Drake and Fielding an announcement that the marriage had taken place. There were letters for both the men, and they carried them out to a grass knoll on the edge of the forest some quarter of a mile away from the little village of tin huts which shone in the sunshine like a tidy kitchen, as Fielding was used to say. Drake read his through, and said to Fielding, 'You have a letter from Mrs. Willoughby?'

'Yes.'

'Any news?'

Fielding looked him in the face. 'Yes,' he said slowly, and putting the letter in his pocket, buttoned it up. Drake understood alike from his tone and action what news the letter conveyed, and made no further inquiry. He fell instead to talking of some machinery which the boat had brought up along with the letters. The letter, indeed, was written in a vein which made it impossible for Fielding to follow the usual habit of reading Mrs. Willoughby's letters aloud to his companion. 'The wedding,' she wrote, 'lacked nothing but a costumier and a composer. The bride and bridegroom should have been in fancy dress, and a new Gounod was needed to compose the wedding-march of a marionette. One might have taken the ceremony seriously as an artistic whole under those circumstances.'

Mrs. Willoughby continued to keep Fielding informed of the progress or the married couple, and in May hinted at dissensions. The hint Fielding let slip one day to Drake. Drake, however, received the news with apparent indifference, and indeed returned to England in September with Fielding without having so much as referred to the subject.

During the month which followed his return, he preserved the same appearance of indifference, seeming, indeed, thoroughly engrossed in working off arrears of business. The fact, however, of this dissension was thrust before his notice one evening when he dined with Mr. Le Mesurier, and that gentleman dealt out extravagant praise to the French for recognising that the marriages of the children are matters which solely concern the parents.

'We English,' said he with a shrug of contempt at the fatuity of his countrymen, 'men and women, or rather boys and girls, choose for ourselves, and what's the result nine times out of ten? Well, it's the custom, and it's no use for a man by himself trying to alter it.'

Drake was familiar with Mr. Le Mesurier's habit of shifting responsibilities, and while he said nothing at the moment, called upon Mrs. Willoughby the next day and questioned her openly. Mrs. Willoughby admitted that there were disagreements, but believed them not to be deep.

'The first year,' she said, 'is as a rule a trying time. There are illusions to be sloughed. People may come out all the stronger in the end.' Mrs. Willoughby generalised to conceal the little hopefulness she felt in regard to the particular instance.

'I ask,' continued Drake, 'because I thought money might be at the bottom of it. In that case something perhaps might be done. Mrs. Mallinson would be troubled, I believe, by a need to economise.'

'Oh no,' she returned. 'There's no trouble of that kind. You see, Mr. Le Mesurier sold the Seigneurie, for one thing—'

'Sold it!' exclaimed Drake. 'Why, I was told that it was strictly entailed from father to child.'

'In one respect it is. It can't be charged with annuities. But any one who owns it can sell it outright. Mr. Le Mesurier always intended to sell it if Clarice married a man only moderately well off.'

Drake rose from his chair and walked once or twice quickly across the room.

'He should have told his daughter that,' he said slowly.

Mrs. Willoughby glanced at him in surprise.

'Well, of course he did.'

'Oh no, he didn't,' said Drake quickly. 'You remember, I told you at Sark why she wanted our engagement to be kept secret.'

'Because your position wasn't altogether assured. You didn't mention the Seigneurie.'

A. E. W. Mason

'No, I thought you would understand. She believed an engagement between us would cause trouble with her father, just because it was necessary for her to marry a man who could keep up the Seigneurie.'

Mrs. Willoughby started. 'Clarice told you that!' she said, staring at him.

'Yes,' he replied simply. 'So you see she didn't know.'

Mrs. Willoughby sank back into her chair. She had heard Mr. Le Mesurier announce his intention more than once in Clarice's presence. However, she fancied that no particular good would be done by informing him of the girl's deception, and she dropped the subject.

'What about Conway?' asked Drake.

'He still walks up and down London. I fancy he is secretary to something.'

Drake hesitated for a second. 'Does he go there very much?'

'A good deal, I fancy,' she replied. 'But you mustn't think the disagreement is really serious. There is no cause outside themselves. Have you called?'

'No; I go down to Bentbridge to-morrow. I must call when I get back.'

'Then you are going to stand for Parliament?' she exclaimed. 'I am so glad.'

'Yes; they expect an election in July, I believe. You see, now that Fielding has been made a director and has settled down to work, I have got more time. In fact, one feels rather lonely at nights.'

Mrs. Willoughby was willing to hear more concerning Fielding's merits. She promptly set herself to belittle the importance of his position and work for the sake of hearing them upheld, and she was not disappointed.

'It's easy enough to laugh at finance, and fashionable into the bargain,' he said. 'But here's the truth of the matter. Money does to-day what was the work of the sword a century or so ago, and, as far as I can see, does it better. To my thinking, it should be held in quite as high esteem. You can put it aside and let it rust if you like, but other nations won't follow your good example. Then the time comes when you must use it, and you find the only men you've got to handle it are the men you can't trust—the bandit instead of the trained soldier. No! Put the best men you can find to finance, I say,' and with that he said good-bye.

'Why doesn't he drop them altogether?' asked Fielding with considerable irritation when Mrs. Willoughby informed him of Drake's intention to renew his acquaintance with the Mallinsons.

'It would only make matters worse if he did,' replied she. 'Clarice would be certain to count any falling off of her friends as a new grievance against her husband.'

'Friends?'

'He is willing to take his place as one.'

'He will find it singularly uninteresting. Friendship between a man and a woman!'

He shrugged his shoulders; then he laughed to himself. Mrs.

A. E. W. Mason

Willoughby got up nervously from her chair and walked to the opposite end of the room.

'These things,' continued Fielding in a perfectly complacent and unconscious tone, 'are best understood by their symbols.'

Mrs. Willoughby swung round. 'Symbols?' she asked curiously.

Fielding took a scat and leaned back comfortably. 'The feelings and emotions,' he began, 'have symbols in the visible world. Of these symbols the greater number are flowers. I won't trouble you with an enumeration of them, for in the first place I couldn't give it, and in the second, Shakespeare has provided a fairly comprehensive list. And by nature I am averse to challenging comparisons. There are, however, feelings of which the symbols are not flowers, and amongst them we must reckon friendship between man and woman. Passion, we know, has its passion flower, but the friendship I am speaking of has its symbol too'—he paused impressively—'and that symbol is cold boiled mutton.'

Mrs. Willoughby laughed awkwardly. 'What nonsense!' she said.

'A mere *jeu d'esprit*, I admit,' said he, and he waved his hand to signify that he could be equally witty every day in the week if he chose. His satisfaction, indeed, blinded him to the fact that his speech might be construed as uncommonly near to a proposal of marriage. He thought, with a cast back to his old dilettante spirit, that it would be amusing to repeat it, especially to a woman of the sentimental kind—Clarice Mallinson, for instance. He pictured the look of injury in her eyes and laughed again.

CHAPTER XII

Clarice was indeed even more disappointed than Mrs. Willoughby imagined. She had looked forward to her marriage, and had indeed been persuaded to look forward to it, as to the smiting of a rock in her husband's nature whence a magical spring of inspiration should flow perennially. 'The future owes us a great deal,' Mallinson had said. 'It does indeed,' Clarice had replied in her most sentimental tones. Only she made the mistake of believing that the date of her marriage was the time appointed for payment. Instead of that spontaneous flow of inspiration, she had beneath her eyes a process of arduous work, which was not limited to a special portion of the day, like the work of a business man, and which, in the case of a man with Mallinson's temperament, inevitably produced an incessant fretfulness with his surroundings. Now, since this work was done not in an office but at home, the burden of that fretfulness fell altogether upon Clarice.

She took to reading the *Morte d'Arthur*. Fielding found her with the book in her hand when he called, and commented on her choice.

'There's no romance in the world nowadays,' she replied.

'But there has been,' he replied cheerfully; 'lots.'

Clarice professed not to understand his meaning. He proceeded to tick off upon his ringers those particular instances in which he knew her to have had a share, and mentioned the names of the gentlemen. He omitted Drake's, however, and Clarice noticed the omission. For the rest she listened quite patiently until he came to an end. Then she asked gravely, 'Do you think that is quite a nice way to talk to a married woman?'

'No,' he admitted frankly, 'I don't.' For a few minutes the conversation lagged.

This was, however, Fielding's first visit since his home-coming, and Clarice yielded to certain promptings of curiosity.

'I hardly expected you would be persuaded to go out to Africa, even by—any one,' she concluded lamely.

'Neither did I,' he replied.

'Did you enjoy it?' she asked.

'I went out a Remus, I return a Romulus.'

There were points in Clarice's behaviour which never failed to excite Fielding's admiration. Amongst these was a habit she possessed of staring steadily into the speaker's face with all the appearance of complete absence of mind whenever an allusion was made which she did not understand, and then continuing the conversation as though the allusion had never been made. 'Of course you had a companion,' she said.

Fielding agreed that he had.

'I have not seen him,' she added.

'No?'

'No.' Clarice was driven to name the companion. 'You seem to have struck up a great friendship with Mr. Drake. I should hardly have thought that you would have found much in common.'

'*Arcades ambo*, don't you know?'

Clarice did not know, and being by this time exasperated, she showed that she did not. Fielding explained blandly, 'We both drive the same pigs to the same market.'

Clarice laughed shortly, and stroked the cover of her *Morte d'Arthur*. 'I suppose that's just what friendship means nowadays?'

'Between man and man—yes. Between woman and woman it's different, and it's, of course, different too between man and woman. But perhaps that's best to be understood by means of its symbol,' and he worked up to his climax of cold boiled mutton with complete satisfaction.

'I gather, then, that you see nothing of Mrs. Willoughby now,' said Clarice quietly as soon as he had stopped. Fielding was for the moment taken aback. It seemed to him that the point of view was unfair. 'Widows,' he replied with great sententiousness,—'widows are different,' and he took his leave without explaining wherein the difference lay. He wondered, however, if Clarice's point of view had occurred to Mrs. Willoughby.

Fielding's visit, and in particular his teasing reticence as to his stay in Matanga, had the effect of recalling Clarice's thoughts to the subject of Stephen Drake. She recalled her old impression of him as one self-centred and self-sufficing, a man to whom nothing outside himself would make any tangible difference; but she recalled it without a trace of the apprehension with which it had been previously coupled. She began indeed to dwell upon that idea of him as upon something restful, and the idea was still prominent in her mind when, a little more than a week afterwards, Drake galloped up to her one morning as she was crossing the Park.

'I have been meaning to call, Mrs. Mallinson,' he said, 'but the fact is, I have had no time. I only got back from Bentbridge last night.'

Clarice received a sudden and yet expected impression of freshness from him. 'Papa told me you were going to stand,' she replied. 'You stayed with my uncle, Captain Le Mesurier, didn't you?'

'Yes. Funnily enough, I have met him before, although I didn't know his name. He travelled in the carriage with me from Plymouth to London when I first landed in England.'

Clarice wondered what made him pause for a moment in the middle of the sentence. 'Your chances are promising?' she asked.

'I can't say yet. I have a Radical lord against me. Burl says there's no opponent more dangerous. It will be a close fight, I think.' He threw back his head and opened his chest. His voice rang with a vigorous enjoyment in the anticipation of a strenuous contest.

'So you are glad to get back to London,' she said.

'Rather. I feel at home here, and only here—even in January.' He looked across the Park with a laugh. It stretched away vacant and dull in the gray cheerlessness of a winter's morning. 'The place fascinates me; it turns me into a child, especially at night. I like the glitter of shops and gas-lamps, and the throng of people in the light of them. One understands what the Roman citizen felt. I like driving about the streets in a hansom. There are some one never gets tired of Oxford Street, for instance, and the turn out of Leicester Square into Coventry Street, with the blaze of Piccadilly Circus ahead. One hears that poets starve in London, and are happy; I can believe it. Well, I am keeping you from the shops, and myself from business.'

He shook hands with her and mounted his horse.

'You have not yet seen my husband,' she said, and she felt that she forced herself to speak the word.

'Not yet. I must look him up. You live in Regent's Park, don't you?'

'Close by. Will you come some evening and dine?'

The invitation was accepted, and Drake rode off. He rode well, Clarice noticed, and his horse was finely limbed and perfectly groomed. The perception of these details had its effect. She stood looking after him, then she turned slowly and made her way homewards across the Park. Two of her acquaintances passed her and lifted their hats, but she took no notice of them; she did not see them. A picture was fixed in her mind—a picture of a rolling plain, black as midnight, exhaling blackness, so that the air itself was black for some feet above the ground; and into this cool and quiet darkness the moonbeams plunged out of a fiery sky and were lost. They dropped, she fancied, after their long flight, to their appointed haven of repose.

The street door of her house gave on to a garden. Clarice

A. E. W. Mason

walked along the pathway in front of the house towards the door of the hall. As she passed her husband's study windows she glanced in. He was standing in front of the fireplace, tearing across some sheets of manuscript. Clarice hurried forwards. He was always tearing up manuscript. While she was upstairs taking off her hat she heard his door open and his voice complaining to the servants about some papers which had been mislaid. She felt inclined to take the servants' part. After all, what was a man doing in the house all day? There was a dragging shuffle of his slippers upon the floor of the hall. The sound jarred on her. She pinned on her hat again, ran downstairs, gave orders that she would not be in for lunch, and drove at once to Mrs. Willoughby's. She arrived in a state little short of hysterical.

'Connie,' she cried, almost before the servant who announced her was out of the room, 'I know you don't like me, but oh, I'm so unhappy!'

Mrs. Willoughby softened at sight of her evident distress. 'Why, what's the matter?' she asked, and made her sit down beside her on the sofa.

'It's awful,' she said, and repeated, 'it's awful.'

'Yes, child, but what is?' asked Mrs. Willoughby.

'All is—I mean everything is,' sobbed Clarice.

Mrs. Willoughby recognised that though the correction amended the grammar, it did not simplify the meaning. She pressed for something more precise.

'Don't be irritable, Connie,' quavered Clarice, 'because that's just what Sidney is—and always. It's so difficult to make you understand. But he's just a lot of wires, and they keep twanging all day. He nags—there's no other word for it—he nags about everything—the servants, his publishers, the dinner, and—oh!—oh!—why can't he wear boots in the morning?'

The point of the question was lost on Mrs. Willoughby. She began to expostulate with Clarice for magnifying trifles.

'Of course,' replied Clarice, sitting up suddenly—she had been half lying on the sofa in Mrs. Willoughby's arms—'I know they are trifles; I know that. But make every day full of them, every day repeat them! Oh, it's awful! I wonder I don't break down!' She turned again to Mrs. Willoughby, lapsing from vehemence to melancholy as the notion occurred to her. 'Connie, I believe I shall—break down altogether. You know I'm not very strong.' She put her arms about Mrs. Willoughby, and clung to her in the intensity of her self-compassion. 'You can't imagine the strain it is. And if that wasn't enough, his mother comes up from Clapham and lectures me. I wouldn't mind that, only she's not very safe about her h's, and she stops to dinner and talks about the nobility she's had cooks from, to impress the servants. It's so humiliating, to be lectured by any one like that.'

Mrs. Willoughby scented a fact. 'But what does she lecture you about? The dinner?' she asked, with an irrelevant recollection of Drake's impression of Clarice as one little adapted for housewifely duties, and not rightly to be troubled by them.

'Oh no. She says I don't give Sidney the help he expected from me. But what more can I do? He has got me. Sidney says the same, too. He told me that he had never had so much difficulty to work properly as since we were married. And when his work doesn't succeed I know he blames me for it. Oh, Connie! *is* it my fault? I think we had better get divorced—and I—I—c-c-can go into a convent, and never do anybody any more harm.'

Clarice glanced as she spoke down the neatest of morning frocks, and the mental picture which she straightway had of herself in a white-washed cell with iron bars, clad in shapeless black, her chin swathed, her face under eaves of starched linen, induced an access of weeping.

For all her sympathy Mrs. Willoughby was forced to bite her lips. Clarice, however, was not in the mood to observe the effect which her words produced on others. She continued: 'It's much the best thing to do, because whatever I did it would always be the same. I could never make him content. Connie, if you only knew the strain of it all! He's always wanting to be something different. One day a clerk, with a nice quiet routine, another a soldier, another a—' she hesitated, and gave Constance an extra squeeze—'a colonist, and fire off Maxim guns. If you could only see him! He sits in front of the fire, with his glasses on, and talks about the roaring world of things.'

This time Mrs. Willoughby really laughed. She turned the laugh into a cough, and cleared her throat emphatically once or twice. Clarice sat up and looked at her reproachfully, then she said, 'I know it's absurd. I don't know whether to laugh or cry myself, b-b-but I usually cry. And then in his books he's—he's always his own hero.' With that Clarice reached at once the climax of her distress and the supreme charge of her indictment. The rest was but sighs and sobs and disconnected phrases. Finally she fell asleep; later she was caressed into eating lunch, taken for a drive, and sent home subsequently greatly mollified and relieved.

Mrs. Willoughby refrained from tendering advice that afternoon. There was nothing sufficiently tangible in the story which she had heard. In fact the only thing really tangible was the girl's distress in telling it, and that Mrs. Willoughby attributed to some dispute between her and Sidney that morning. She could not know that Clarice's outburst had been preceded by that chance meeting in the Park with Stephen Drake, for Clarice had made no allusion to it of any kind. She felt, besides, that advice in any case would be of little use. The couple had to work out their own salvation, and time and experience alone could help them. Events seemed to justify Mrs. Willoughby's reticence, for the winter blossomed into spring, the spring flowered into summer, and the Mallinson household remained to the external view unshaken.

Drake's visits to Bentbridge increased in frequency as the prospect of the general election became more real. A snap vote in the House of Commons on a minor question of administrative expenditure decided the matter suddenly towards the end of June. The Government determined on a dissolution. Fielding took Clarice Mallinson into dinner at Mr. Le Mesurier's house on the day after the date of the dissolution was fixed. He noticed that she looked worn. There were shadows about her eyes, her colour had lost its freshness, and there was a melancholy droop about the corners of her mouth. Fielding suggested the advisability of a change.

'I'm to have one,' said she. 'I'm going down to stay with my uncle at Bentbridge in a week's time.'

'At Bentbridge?' asked Fielding sharply. 'For the election.'

She saw his lips tighten. 'My husband goes with me,' she replied quickly and stopped, flushing as she realised that she had meant and conveyed an apology.

'I should have thought that the Continent would have been more advisable as a change.'

'The Continent! I don't want to travel far. I am so tired.' She spoke in a tone of weariness which touched Fielding in spite of himself. He looked at her more closely. 'Yes,' he said gently, 'you look very tired. You have been doing too much.'

'No, it isn't that,' she replied. 'One thinks of things, that's all.' She bent her head and was silent for a little, tracing a pattern on the table-cloth with a finger absently. Then she added in a low voice, 'I suppose few women ever think at all until after they are married.'

The voice was low, and Fielding was conscious of something new in the tone of it, a deeper vibration, a sincerity different in kind from that surface frankness which he had always known in her. He wondered whether she had struck down from her pinchbeck sentimentality into something that rang solid in the depths of her nature. He looked at her again, her eyes were turned to his. With the shadows about them, they looked bigger, darker, more piteously appealing. She was no less a child to him, the child looked out of her eyes, sounded in the commonplace sentiment she had spoken, and the air of originality with which she had spoken it. But the child seemed beginning to learn the lesson of womanhood, and from the one mistress which could teach it her.

'But why think then?' he asked lightly. 'It ruins a complexion no less than before. Or does a complexion cease to count? Look!' He leaned forward. A pink carnation was in a glass in front of him, already withering from the heat. He touched the faded tips of the petals. 'That is the colour which conies from thinking.'

Clarice lifted her shoulders with more of sadness than impatience in the gesture. 'You believe,' she said, 'no woman at all has a right to dare to think.'

'I notice,' he answered with the same levity, 'that the woman who thinks generally thinks of what she ought not to.'

Later, in the drawing-room, he looked for her again, and looked unsuccessfully. The window, however, was open, and he advanced to it. Clarice was on the balcony alone, her elbows on the rail, a hand on either side of her cheek. Something in her attitude made him almost pity her.

'Mrs. Mallinson,' he said, 'you will probably think me intrusive, but do you think your visit really wise?' Clarice turned towards him quickly with something of defiance in her manner. 'You are tired,' he went on, 'you want rest. Well, an election isn't a very restful time, even for the onlooker.'

Clarice did not reply for a moment, and when she did she replied with an impulsive frankness, to which his friendly tone had prompted her. 'To tell you the truth, I am not anxious to go. I don't want to, but Sidney wants to.'

'Your husband?'

'You don't believe me.'

'Of course I do.' He left her on the balcony, and went in search of Mallinson. 'So you go to Bentbridge for the election,' he said.

'Yes,' replied the other, lighting up. 'I am looking forward to it like a schoolboy to a football match. The prospect of activity exhilarates me—bodily activity, don't you know—a town humming with excitement.'

Fielding cut him short. 'My dear fellow, you're a damned fool,' he said.

CHAPTER XIII

Stephen Drake had decided to stay during the period of the election at a hotel in the centre of the town, rather than to accept an invitation from Captain Le Mesurier, who lived some miles beyond the outskirts. He travelled down to Bentbridge on the day that the dissolution was announced, and during the journey Mr. Burl gave him much sage advice.

'Keep the arguments for buildings; they're in place there. Mass-meetings in the open air want something different. Many a good man has lost his seat from not observing that rule. In the open air pitch out a fact or two—not too many— or a couple of round sums of figures first of all, just to give them confidence in you, and then go straight for your opponent. No rapier play—it's lost then—but crack him on the top-knot with a bludgeon. They'll want to hear his skull ring before they'll believe that you have touched him. Phrases! Those are the things to get you in, not arguments. Pin a label on his coat-tails. You'll see them laugh as he squirms round to pull it off. And, mind you, there'll be no walking over, you'll want all you know. The man's a Radical and a Lord! The combination satisfies their democratic judgments and their snobbish instincts at the same time. People forget to count the snob in the democrat, but he's there all the same, as in most Englishmen. A veneer of snobbishness over solid independence. That's our characteristic. Lord Cranston! Can't you hear their tongues licking it? Luckily, there are things against him. He's a carpet-bagger like yourself, and he's been more than once separated from his wife. His fault, too—once it was an opera dancer. I've got up the facts. He only joined his wife again a few months ago—probably for the purpose of this election.'

Mr. Burl pulled out a pocket-book, and began to turn over the leaves in search of the damning details, when Drake interrupted him. 'You don't expect me to discuss the man's private life?'

'My dear Drake, do be practical. It's no use being finicking. The essential thing is to win the seat.'

'Whatever the price?'

'Look here; I am not asking you to do anything so crude as to make platform speeches about the man's disgraceful conduct to his wife.' Mr. Burl assumed the look of a Rhadamanthus. 'But'—and again he relaxed into the tactician—'you might take a strong social line on morals generally, and the domestic hearth, and that sort of thing.' He looked critically at Drake. 'You're one of the few chaps I know who look as if they could do that and make people believe they really mean it.'

He finally discredited his advice by adding impressibly, 'You needn't go into the instance at all, you know. They'll understand what you're alluding to, never fear'; and Drake flatly refused to dance into Parliament to that tune, however persuasively Mr. Burl played upon the pipes.

The hotel at which Drake put up was situated in a short broad street which ran from the Market Square. From the balcony of his sitting-room on the first floor he could see the market sheds at the end of the street to his left. The opposite end was closed in by the Town Hall, which was built upon an ancient gate of the town. From Drake's windows you got a glimpse through the archway of green fields and trees. Almost facing him was a second hotel on the opposite side of the street, the 'Yellow Boar.' It was tricked out, he noticed, with the colours of his opponent. While he was standing at the window an open carriage turned out of the market-place, and drove up to the 'Yellow Boar.' Lord Cranston got down from it, and a lady. The candidate was of a short and slight build; a pencil—line of black moustache crossed a pallid and indecisive face, and he seemed a year or two more than thirty. The lady looked the younger, and was certainly the taller of the two. Drake was impressed by her face, which bore womanly gentleness, stamped on features of a marked intellectuality. The couple disappeared into the hall, and appeared again in a large room with big windows upon the first floor. From where he stood Drake could see every corner of the room. Lord and Lady Cranston, the land-lord informed him, were staying at the 'Yellow Boar.' The two candidates overlooked each other.

In this street, morning and evening, they met for a moment or two, and took a breath of friendly intercourse. Drake was introduced to Lady Cranston, but she would have none of the truce. To her he was the enemy, and to be treated as such consistently, with a heart-and-soul hostility, until he confessed himself beaten. Drake liked her all the better for her attitude. Meanwhile he made headway in the consti-tuency. He was in earnest, with a big theme to descant upon—the responsibility of the constituency to the empire. His fervour brought it home to his audiences as a fact; he set the recognition of that responsibility forwards as the prime duty of the citizen, sneering at the parochial notion of politics. Mr. Burl shook his head over Drake's method of fighting the battle, and hinted more than once at the necessity of that lecture upon morals. Drake not only refused to reconsider it, but flatly forbade Mr. Burl to allude to the subject in any speech which he might make. Burl shrugged his shoulders and confided his doubts to Captain Le Mesurier. Said the Captain, 'I think he's wise; a speech might offend. What's wanted is an epigram—a good stinging epigram. We could set it about, and, if it's sharp enough, no need to fear it won't travel.' He paused dubiously. 'After all, though, it's a bit unfair on Cranston. Hang it, I've been a married man myself,' and he chuckled in unregenerate enjoyment. 'However, the seat's got to be won. Let's think of an epigram,' and he scratched his head and slapped his thigh. It was the Captain's way of thinking. The satisfactory epigram would not emerge. He could fashion nothing better as a description of Cranston than, 'A refreshment-room sandwich; two great chunks of sin and a little slice of repentance between.' Mr. Burl condemned it as crude, and for the moment the epigram was dropped.

The Mallinsons arrived a week after the contest had begun. Captain Le Mesurier welcomed Clarice with boisterous effusion, and her husband with quarter-deck dignity. 'You look ill,' he said to Clarice. 'It's your husband worrying you. Ah, I know, I know! Those writing chaps!'

To Mallinson, however, he suddenly showed excessive friendliness, and took the opportunity of saying to him loudly in a full room, 'There's something I must tell you. I know it'll make you laugh. It does me whenever I think of it. You know Drake? Well, we travelled up from Plymouth together when he came back from Africa. He bought your book at the bookstall, and sat opposite me reading it. What was it called? I know, *A Man of Influence*. You should have seen Drake's face. Lord, he couldn't make head or tail of it. How should he? I asked him what he thought of it, and imagine what he answered! You can't, though. It's the funniest thing I ever heard. He said it was a very clever satire. Satire! Good Lord, I almost rolled off the seat. It is funny, isn't it?'

Mallinson, with a wry face, agreed that the story was funny.

'I knew you would think so,' pursued the Captain relentlessly. 'Everybody does I have told it to, and that's everybody I know. Satire! Lord help us!' and he shook with laughter and clapped Mallinson in the small of the back.

Mallinson felt the fool that he was intended to look, with the result that his dormant resentment against Drake sprang again into activity. That resentment became intensified, as the date of the election drew nearer, by an unconfessed jealousy. They both made speeches, but Mallinson chiefly at the smaller meetings. And when they stood upon the same platform he was continually forced to compare the difference in the acclamation with which their speeches were severally received. As a matter of fact, Drake spoke from a fire of conviction, and the conviction not merely burnt through his words, but minted them for him, gave him spontaneously the short homely phrase which sank his meaning into the minds of his hearers. Mallinson took refuge in a criticism of Drake's speeches from the standpoint of literary polish. He recast them in his thoughts, turning this sentence more deftly, whittling that repartee to a finer point. The process consoled him for Drake's misreckoning of his purpose in the matter of *A Man of Influence*, since it pointed to a certain lack of delicacy, say at once to crassness in the man's intellect.

Mallinson began immediately to imagine himself in Drake's position, the candidate for whom brass bands played, and hats went spinning into the air. And it needed no conscious effort for one so agile in egotistical leaps to spring thence to the fancy that Drake was a kind of vicarious substitute for himself, doing his work, too, not without blemishes.

Ten days before the polling-day Fielding ran down from town, and attended a meeting at the Town Hall, at which both Drake and Mallinson were to speak. He sat on the platform by Clarice's side and paid some attention to her manner during the evening. He noticed the colour mount in her cheeks and her eyes kindle, as on first entering the room she looked down upon the crowded floor. The chairs had been removed, and the audience stood packed beneath the flaring gas-jets—artificers for the most part, their white faces smeared and stained with the grime of their factories. The roar of applause as Drake rose by the table swelled up to three cheers in consonance, and a subsequent singing of 'For he's a jolly good fellow' stirred even Fielding to enthusiasm. He noted that feeling of enthusiasm as strange in himself, and had a thought in consequence that such scenes were hardly of the kind to help Clarice to the rest she needed. The hall for a moment became a sea of tossing handkerchiefs. He took a glance at Clarice. She sat bent forward with parted lips and a bosom that heaved. Fielding turned on his cold-water tap of flippancy.

'It's a bad omen,' said he, with a nod towards the waving handkerchiefs. 'They hang out flags of surrender.'

'Hardly,' she replied, with a smile. 'I can't recognise that the flags are white'; and she added, 'I should like it less if they were. These men are the workers.'

'The workers.' Fielding could hear Drake uttering the word in just the same tone, and his compassion for Clarice deepened. Why? he asked himself. The girl was undergoing not a jot more punishment than a not over-rigid political justice would have meted out to her. The question inexplicably raised to view a pair of the clearest blue eyes, laughing from between the blackest of eyelashes. He promptly turned his attention to the speaker at the table.

Drake commenced that night with an apology. It was necessary that he should speak about himself. An utterly baseless story had, within the last few days, and doubtless with a view to this election, been revived by the London evening paper which originally made it. He regretted also to notice that his opponent had accepted the story, and was making use of it to prejudice him in the eyes of the electors. Accordingly he felt bound to put the facts simply and briefly before his audience, although the indifference of the Colonial Office to what, if true, was a crime committed by an Englishman on English soil, and against practically English subjects, in effect acquitted him of the charge.

Drake thereupon proceeded to describe his march to Boruwimi. The story, modestly recited in simple nervous English, did more to forward his candidature than all the political speeches he could have made during a twelvemonth. It came pat at the right time, when arguments were growing stale. His listeners hung upon the words; in the intense silence Fielding could feel the sympathy between speaker and audience flowing to and fro between them like a current. Drake instinctively lowered his voice; it thrilled through the hall the more convincingly. There was a perceptible sway of heads forwards, which started at the back and ran from line to line towards the platform like a quick ripple across a smooth sea. It was as though this crowded pack of men and women was drawn to move towards the speaker, where indeed there was no room at all to move.

And in truth the subject was one to stir the blood. Drake prefaced his account by a description of the geography of Boruwimi; he instanced briefly the iniquities of the Arab slave-dealers whom he was attacking. Thereupon he contrasted the numbers of his little force with the horde of his enemies, and dwelt for a second upon their skill as marksmen; so that his auditors, following him as he hewed

A. E. W. Mason

his path through the tangle of an untrodden forest, felt that each obstacle he stopped at might mean not merely failure to the expedition, but death to all who shared in it. Success and life were one and the same thing, and the condition of that thing was speed. He must fall upon the Arabs unawares, like a bolt from the blue. They forgot that he who led that expedition was speaking to them now; they were with him in the obscure depths of the undergrowth, surging against gigantic barriers of fallen tree-trunks, twenty, thirty feet high; they were marching behind him, like him at grips with nature in a six-weeks' struggle of life and death; and when finally he burst into the clearing on the river's bank the ripple went backwards across the hall, and a cheer of relief rang out, as though their lives, too, were saved.

Upon Fielding the relation produced a somewhat peculiar effect. He was fascinated, not so much by the incident described or by the earnestness of the man who described it,—for with both he was familiar,—but by the strangeness of the conditions under which it was told—this story of Africa, before these serried rows of white eager faces, in this stifling hall, where the gaslight struggled with the waning day. From the raised platform on which he sat he could see through the open windows away across green fields to where the sun was setting in a clear sky behind quiet Yorkshire wolds. The combination of circumstances made the episode bizarre to him; he was, in fact, paying an unconscious tribute to the orator's vividness.

Clarice paid the same tribute, but she phrased it differently, and the difference was significant. She said, 'Isn't it strange that he should *be here*—in a frock-coat? I half thought the room would dissolve and we should find ourselves at Boruwimi.' Fielding started. Coming from her lips the name sounded strange; yet she spoke it without the least hesitation. For the moment it had plainly one association in her thoughts, and only one. It sounded as though every recollection of Gorley had vanished from her mind. 'Oh, he must get in!' she whispered, clasping her hands upon her knees.

After Drake had concluded, Mallinson moved a resolution. He spoke fluently, Fielding remarked, and with a finished phrasing. The very finish, however, imparted an academic effect; he was, besides, hampered by the speech which had preceded his. The audience began to shuffle restlessly; they were capping a rich Burgundy with *vin ordinaire*, and found the liquor tasteless to the palate. Fielding perceived from certain movements at his side that Clarice shared in the general restlessness. She gave an audible sigh of relief and patted her hands with the most perfunctory applause when her husband sat down. 'You are staying with Mr. Drake at the Three Nuns?' she asked, turning to Fielding.

'Only till to-morrow. I leave by the night-train.'

'Oh, you are going back!'

'Yes. You see Drake and Burl are both here. Somebody must keep the shop open, if it's only to politely put the customers off.' He interpreted the look of surprise upon Mrs. Mallinson's face. 'Yes, I have been gradually sucked into the whirlpool,' and he laughed with a nod towards Drake.

She turned to him with her eyes shining. 'And you are proud of it.'

Fielding smiled indulgently. 'That's a woman's thought.'

'But you don't deny it's truth.'

Clarice said nothing more until the meeting had terminated and the party was in the street. They walked from the Town

Hall to Drake's hotel, Clarice and Fielding a few paces behind the rest. The first words which she spoke showed to him that her thoughts had not altered their drift. 'Yes, you have changed,' she said, and implied unmistakably, 'for the better.'

'You only mean,' laughed Fielding, 'that I have given up provoking you.'

'No, no,' she said. 'Besides, you evidently haven't given that up.'

'Then in what way?'

'I shall offend you.'

'I can hardly think so.'

'Well, you were becoming a kind of—'

'Say it.'

'Paul Pry.'

To a gentleman whose ambition it had been to combine the hermit's indifference to social obligations with an indulgence in social festivities, the blow was a cruel one; and the more cruel because he realised that Clarice's criticism contained a grain of truth. He hit back cruelly. 'Drake tells me he thinks of taking a place here. I suppose he means to marry.'

'I believe he does,' replied Clarice promptly. 'Mrs. Willoughby.'

Fielding stopped and apostrophised the stars. 'That is perfectly untrue,' he said. He walked on again as soon as he perceived that he had stopped, adding, with a grumble, 'I pity the woman who marries Drake.'

'Why?' asked Clarice in a tone of complete surprise, as though the idea was incomprehensible to her, and she repeated insistently, 'Why?'

'Well,' he said, inventing a reason, 'I think he would never stand in actual need of her.' Clarice drew a sharp breath—a sigh of longing, it seemed to her companion, as for something desirable beyond all blessings. He continued in the tone of argument, 'And she would come to know that. Surely she would feel it.'

'Yes, but feel proud of it perhaps,' replied Clarice, 'proud of him just for that reason. All her woman's tricks she would know useless to move him. Nothing she could do would make him swerve. Oh yes, she would feel proud—proud of him and proud of herself because he stooped to choose her.' She corrected the ardency of her voice of a sudden; it dropped towards indifference. 'At all events I can imagine that possible.'

They were within fifty yards of the hotel, and walked silently the rest of the way. At the door, however, she said, turning weary eyes upon Fielding, 'And think! The repose of it for her.'

'Ah, here you are!' The robustious voice of Captain Le Mesurier sounded from the hall. 'Look here,' to Fielding, 'we are going to take you back with us. Drake won't come. He's tired—so we don't miss him.'

Fielding protested vainly that he would crowd the waggonette. Besides, he had business matters to discuss with Drake before he left for London.

'Well, you can talk them over to-morrow. You don't go until to-morrow night. And as to crowding the waggonette, I have ordered a trap here; so you can drive it back again to-night, if you like, from Garples. Otherwise we'll be happy to put you up. You must come; we want to talk to you particularly. Mallinson will drive his wife in the trap, so there'll be plenty of room.'

The party in the waggonette consisted of Captain Le Mesurier, Burl, Fielding, and five country gentlemen belonging to the district. Clarice, riding some yards behind them through the dark fragrant lanes, saw eight glowing cigars draw together in a bunch. The cigars were fixed points of red light for a little. Then they danced as though heads were wagging, retired this side and that and set to partners. A minute more and the figure was repeated: cigars to the centre, dance, retire, set to partners. A laugh from the Captain sounded as though he laughed from duty, and Mr. Burl was heard to say, 'Not too subtle, old man, you know.' At the third repetition the Captain bellowed satisfaction from a full heart, and Mr. Burl cried, 'Capital!' The country gentlemen could be understood to agree in the commendation. Whence it was to be inferred that the dance of the cigars was to have a practical result upon the election.

Clarice, however, paid no great attention to the proceedings in the waggonette. She was almost oblivious to the husband at her side. The night was about her, cool with soft odours, wrapping her in solitude. Love at last veritably possessed her, so she believed; it had invaded her last citadel to-night. That it sat throned on ruins she had no eyes to see. It sat throned in quiescence, and that was enough. Clarice, in fact, was in that compressed fever-heat of the mushroom passions which takes on the semblance of intense and penetrating calm. And her very consciousness of this calm seemed to ally her to Drake, to give to them both something in common. She was troubled by no plans for the future; she had no regret for anything which had happened in the past. The vague questions which had stirred her—why had she been afraid of him?—was the failure of her marriage her fault?—for these questions she had no room. She did not think at all, she only felt that her heart was anchored to a rock.

A. E. W. Mason

CHAPTER XIV

Given a driver who is at once inexperienced and short-sighted, a fresh horse harnessed to a light dog-cart, a dark night and a narrow gateway, and the result may be forecast without much rashness. Mallinson upset his wife and the cart just within the entrance to Garples. Luckily the drive was bordered by thick shrubs of laurel, so that Clarice was only shaken and dazed. She sat in the middle of a bush vaguely reflecting that her heart was anchored to a rock and yet her husband had spilled her out of a dog-cart. Between the incident and her state of mind immediately preceding it, she recognised an incongruity which she merely felt to be in some way significant. Fielding and Captain Le Mesurier picked her out of the bush before she had time to examine into its significance. All she said was, 'It's so like him.'

'Yes, hang the fellow!' said the Captain, and under his breath he launched imprecations at all 'those writer chaps.'

Mallinson raised himself from a bed of mould upon the opposite side of the drive and apologised. Captain Le Mesurier bluntly cut short the apology. 'Why didn't you say you couldn't drive? I can't. Who's ashamed of it? You might have broken your wife's neck.'

'I might, and my own too,' replied Mallinson in a tone not a whit less aggrieved.

Captain Le Mesurier raised his eyes to the heavens with the apoplectic look which comes of an intense desire to swear, and the repressive presence of ladies. 'Will you kindly sit on the horse's head until you are told to get up? I want the groom to help here,' he said, as soon as he found words tolerable to feminine ears. A groom was already occupying the position designated, but he rose with alacrity and Mallinson silently took his place and sat there until the harness was loosed.

Fielding's visit, however, had another consequence beyond the upsetting of a gig. A few days later an epigram was circulating through the constituency. The squires passed it on with a smack of the tongue; it had a flavour, to their thinking, which was of the town. The epigram was this: 'Lord Cranston lives a business life of vice, with rare holidays of repentance, but being a dutiful husband he always takes his wife with him on his holidays.' From the squires it descended through the grades of society. Lord Cranston, at the close of a speech, was invited to mention the precise date at which he intended to end his holidays. Believing that the question sprang out of an objection to a do-nothing aristocracy, he answered with emphatic earnestness, 'The moment I am returned for Bentbridge.' The shout of laughter which greeted the remark he attributed at first to political opposition.

Subsequently, however, a sympathiser explained to him delicately the true meaning of the question, and, as a counter-move, Lord Cranston made a violent attack upon 'Empire building plus finance.' He drew distinctions between governing men and making money.

Drake accepted the distinctions as obvious platitudes, but

A. E. W. Mason

failed to see that the capacity for one could not coexist with the capacity for the other. He asserted, on the contrary, that money was not as a rule made without the exercise of tact, and some aptitude for the management of men. He was, consequently, not disinclined to believe that money-making afforded a good preliminary lesson in the art of government. Lord Cranston's argument, in fact, did little more then alienate a few of his own supporters, who, having raised themselves to affluence, felt quite capable of doing the same for the nation.

On the night of the polling-day Captain Le Mesurier brought his house-party into Bentbridge to dine with Drake, and after dinner the ladies remained in the room overlooking the street, while the gentlemen repaired to the Town Hall, where the votes were being counted. It seemed to Clarice as she gazed down that all the seven thousand electors had gathered to hear the result announced. The street was paved with heads as with black cobble-stones. Occasionally some one would look up and direct now a cheer, now a shout of derision towards the 'Three Nuns' or the 'Yellow Boar.' But the rooms of both candidates were darkened, and the attention of the crowd was for the most part riveted upon the red blinds of the Town Hall.

For Clarice, the time limped by on crutches. She barely heard the desultory conversation about her: she felt as if her life was beating itself out against those red windows. A clock in the market-place chimed the hour of nine: she counted the strokes, with a sense of wonder when they stopped. She seemed to have been waiting for a century.

Across the street she could see the glimmer of a light summer dress in Lord Cranston's apartment. It moved restlessly backwards and forwards from one window to the other: now it shone out in the balcony above the street: now it retired into the darkness of the room. Clarice gauged Lady Cranston's impatience by her own, and experienced a fellow-feeling of sympathy. 'During this suspense,' she thought, 'you and I ought to be together.' As the thought flashed into her mind, her husband spoke to her. She set a hand before her eyes and did not answer him. She realised that she had been thinking of herself as Drake's wife. On the instant every force within her seemed to concentrate and fuse into one passionate longing. 'If only that were true!' She felt the longing throb through every vein: she acknowledged it: she expressed it clearly to herself. If only that were true! And then in a second the longing was displaced by an equally passionate regret.

'It might have been,' she thought.

Again her husband spoke to her. She turned towards him almost fiercely, and saw that he was offering her a shawl. She steadied her voice to decline it, and turned back again to the window. But now as she looked across the street, she was filled with a new and very bitter envy. The woman over there had the right to suffer for her suspense.

At last the clock doled out ten strokes with a grudging deliberation, and less than five minutes later the shadow of a man was seen upon one of the red blinds. In the street below the people surged forward: there was a running flash of white as their heads were thrown back and their faces upturned to the Hall; and the shouts and cries swelled to a Babel, tearing the air. The blind was withdrawn, the window thrown open: Clarice could see people pressing forward in the room. They looked in the glare of yellow light like black ninepins. A gleam of bright scarlet shot out from amongst them, and the Mayor stepped on to the balcony above the archway. The tumult died rapidly to absolute silence, a silence deeper than the silence of desolate places, because

A. E. W. Mason

one saw the crowd and one's ears were still tingling with the echo of its shouts. It was as though all sound, all motion had been arrested by some enchantment, and in the midst of that silence one word was launched down the street.

'Drake!'

The announcement of the numbers was lost in the sudden renewal of conflicting shouts. Clarice made no effort to ascertain them. That one word 'Drake' filled the world for her. The very noise in the street came to her ears with a dull muffled sound as though it had travelled across a wide space, and it seemed no more than an undertone to the ringing name.

She saw Stephen Drake come forward and give place to his opponent, and after a little the street began to clear. The number thirty-five, incessantly repeated by the retiring crowd, penetrated to her mind and informed her of the actual majority. In about half an hour a little stream of people trickled from the porch of the Town Hall, and, gathering in volume, flowed into a narrow passage which led to the Conservative Club, a few yards to the right of the hotel. Clarice caught a glimpse of Drake's face at the head of the procession as he passed under a gas-lamp above the mouth of the passage, and was surprised by its expression of despondency. A fear sprang up in her mind that some mistake had been made in the announcement, but the fear was dispelled by the tone of her uncle's voice as he shouted an invitation to some one across the street to join them at the Club. It was a tone of boisterous exultation. There could be no doubt that Drake had been elected, and she wondered at the cause of his dejection.

A few minutes later a second stream flowed along the opposite pavement towards the Liberal Club in the Market

Square, and drew most of the remaining loiterers into its current. The noise and bustle grew fainter and died away: the lights were extinguished in the houses, and only one small group, clustering excitedly about the passage, relieved the quarter of its native sleepiness.

Clarice turned with a certain reluctance into the room. It was empty, and the voices of her companions rose from the hall below. She did not follow them, however. There was time enough, for the party could not leave until Captain Le Mesurier returned from the Conservative Club. She went back to her post. Through the open window opposite to her she perceived the glimmer of a light dress in the dark of the room, but it was motionless now, a fixed patch of white. Clarice experienced a revulsion of pity for Lady Cranston. 'What must be her thoughts?' she asked herself.

She remained at the window until the party from the Club emerged again from the passage and turned towards the hotel.

Clarice heard her husband's voice asking where Drake was, and what in the world was the matter with him. Captain Le Mesurier replied, and the reply rang boisterously. 'He's behind. He's a bit unstrung, I fancy, and reason enough too, after all his work, eh? You see, Drake's not in the habit of taking holidays,' and the Captain grew hilarious over his allusion.

Across the street Clarice saw the light dress flutter and move abruptly. It was evident that Lady Cranston had heard and understood the words.

Drake followed some few minutes later, and alone. He walked slowly to the hotel with an air of utter weariness, as though the springs of his activity had been broken. A moment after, he had entered it; she heard him ascending the staircase, and she drew instinctively close within the curtains. He pushed open the door, walked forward into the embrasure of the window, and stood within a foot of Clarice, apparently gazing into the street. A pale light from the gas-lamp over the front door flickered upon his face. It was haggard and drawn, the lips were pressed closely together, the eyelids shut tightly over the eyes—a white mask of pain. Or was this the real face, Clarice wondered, and that which he showed to the world the mask?

She was almost afraid to move; she even held her breath.

Suddenly the echoes of the street were reawakened. Drake roused himself and opened his eyes. A small group of people strolled out of the market-place and stopped in front of the 'Yellow Boar.' There was interchange of farewells, a voice said encouragingly, 'Better luck next time,' and one man entered the hotel.

In the room opposite a match flared up and Lady Cranston lit the gas. She stood for a moment underneath the chandelier, in the full light, listening. Then she walked quickly to the mirror above the mantelpiece and appeared to dry her eyes and cheeks with her handkerchief. She turned to the door almost guiltily, just as it opened. Lord Cranston advanced into the room, and his wife moved towards him. The whole scene, every movement, every corner of the room was visible to Clarice like a scene on the stage of a theatre; it was visible also to Drake.

Clarice could note the disconsolate attitude of Lord Cranston, the smile of tenderness upon his wife's face. She saw Lady Cranston set her arms gently about his neck, and her lips move, and then a low hoarse cry burst from Drake at her side.

It sounded to her articulate with all the anguish and all the suffering of which she had ever heard. There was a harsh note of irony in it too, which deepened its sadness. It seemed almost an acknowledgment of defeat in the actual moment of victory—a recognition that after all his opponent had really won.

The cry was a revelation to Clarice; it struck her like a blow, and she started under it, so that the rings of the curtain rattled upon the pole.

Drake bent sharply towards her; she caught a gleam of his eyes in the darkness. Then with a catch of his breath he started back. Clarice heard the click of a match-box, the scraping of a lucifer, and Drake held the lighted match above his head.

'You!' he said.

Clarice moved out from the curtain and confronted him. She did not answer, and he did not speak again. Clarice was in no doubt as to the meaning of his cry. His eyes even in that unsteady light told it to her only too clearly.

And this was the man whom she had believed to stand in no need of a woman's companionship. The thought at the actual moment of its occurrence sent a strange thrill of disappointment through her; she had built up her pride in him so confidently upon this notion of his independence. And having built up her pride, she had lived in it, using this very notion as her excuse and justification. She ran no risk, she had felt.

'Clarice!'

The name was shouted impatiently from the hall, and came

A. E. W. Mason

to them quite audibly through the half-opened door. But neither she nor Drake seemed to hear it. They stood looking silently into each other's eyes.

At last she began to speak, and as she spoke, her sense of disappointment diminished and died. She became conscious again of the suffering which his cry had confessed. The contrast between this one outburst and his ordinary self-control enforced its meaning upon her. It seemed still to be ringing in her ears, stretched out to a continuous note, and her voice gradually took a tone as of one pleading for forgiveness.

'I did not know,' she said. 'I always thought of you as—' and she gave a queer little laugh, 'as driving about London in hansoms, and working quite contentedly. I never imagined that you cared at all—really, I mean, as I know now. Even right at the beginning—that afternoon in Beaufort Gardens, I never imagined that. Indeed, I was afraid of you.'

'Afraid!' Drake echoed the word with an accent of wonderment.

'Yes, yes, afraid. I believed that I should mean so little to you, that I should be of no use or help to you. And that's why I—I—married—'

Drake straightened his shoulders with a jerk as Clarice uttered the word. He became aware of the tell-tale look in his eyes, and lowered them from the girl's face to the ground.

'You mustn't fancy,' he began in a hesitating tone. 'You mustn't misunderstand. I was thinking what men owe to women—that's all—that's all, indeed—and how vilely they repay it. That way, like Cranston'—he nodded in the direction of the house across the street—'or worse—or worse,' he clung to the word on a lift of his voice, as though he found some protection in it, as though he appealed to Clarice to agree with and second him, 'or worse.'

The match burned down to his fingers, and he dropped it on the floor and set his foot on it. Once in the darkness he repeated 'or worse,' with a note almost of despair, and then he was silent. Clarice simply waited. She stood, feeling the darkness throb about her, listening to the sharp irregular breathing which told her where Drake stood. In a few moments he stirred, and she stretched out her hands towards him. But again she heard the click of a match-box, and again the thin flame of light flared up in the room.

'Clarice!'

Her name was shouted up a second time. There was a sound of quicker footsteps upon the stairs, the door was flung back, and Sidney Mallinson entered the room. Drake lighted the gas.

'We have been waiting for you,' said Mallinson to his wife. 'I couldn't think where you had got to,' and he glanced from her to Drake.

'I have been here all the time,' she said with a certain defiance.

Mallinson turned and walked down the stairs again, without as much as a word to Drake. Clarice followed him, and after her came Drake.

'Ah, here you are!' said Captain Le Mesurier. 'Now we're ready. Drake, you are coming back with us?'

Drake hesitated.

'You said you would at the Town Hall. So I have had your bag packed, and put in the waggonette.'

'Very well,' he assented; and the party went outside the hotel.

'Now, how shall we go?' asked the Captain. 'Mallinson, you of course in the waggonette,' and he chuckled with a cheery maliciousness. 'Clarice, will you get in?'

'No!' she said with an involuntary vehemence. The idea of driving back wedged in amongst a number of people, listening to their chatter, and forced to take her share in it, became suddenly repugnant to her. 'I would rather drive in the trap, if I might.'

'Very well! But who is to drive you?' Captain Le Mesurier turned to Drake. 'You can drive, of course.'

Drake replied absently. 'I have driven the coach from Johannesburg to Pretoria, ten mules and a couple of ponies, and a man beside you swinging a sixty-foot lash.'

Captain Le Mesurier laughed out. 'Then there'll be no upset to-night. Come along.'

The guests took their seats, while Drake stood on the pavement.

'Come along, Drake,' shouted the Captain from the box seat of the waggonette.

Drake roused himself with a start. 'I beg your pardon,' he said, and he went to the side of the dog-cart. He drew back when he saw Clarice already in it, and looked from cart to waggonette. 'I am so sorry,' he said in a low voice. 'I was not listening, I am afraid.'

He mounted beside her, whipped up the horse, and drove ahead of the waggonette. They passed out of the town into the open country. Behind them the sounds of wheels grew fainter and fainter and died away. In front the road gleamed through the night like a white riband; the hedgerows flung out a homely scent of honeysuckle and wild roses; above, the stars rode in a clear sky. To Clarice this was the perfect hour of her life. All her speculations had dropped from her; she had but one thought, that this man driving her cared for her, as she cared for him. It was, in truth, more than a thought; she felt it as a glory about her. Accidentally, as the trap swung round a bend of the road, she leaned her weight upon his arm and she felt the muscles brace beneath his sleeve. The sensation confirmed her thought, and she repeated her action deliberately and more than once. She had but one wish, that this drive should never end, that they should go forward always side by side through a starlit night, in a stillness unbroken by the sound of voices. And that wish was more a belief than a wish.

They ascended the slope and came out upon an open moor. It stretched around them, dark with heather as far as they could see. The night covered it like a tent. It seemed the platform of the world. Clarice suddenly recollected her old image of the veld, and she laughed at the recollection as one laughs at some queer fancy one has held in childhood.

Across the moor the wind blew freshly into their faces. Drake quickened the horse's paces, and Clarice imagined a lyrical note in the ringing beat of its hooves. The road dipped towards a valley. A stream wound along the bed of it, and as they reached the crest of the moor they could see below them the stars mirrored in the stream. Upon one of the banks a factory was built, and its six tiers of windows were so many golden spots of light like the flames of candles. Drake stopped the trap and sat watching the factory.

A. E. W. Mason

'Night and day,' he said, 'night and day. There is no end to it. It is the law.'

He spoke not so much dispiritedly, but rather as though he was teaching himself a lesson which he must needs surely get by heart. He lifted the reins and drove down the hill, past the factory and along the valley to the gates of Garples. There he stopped the trap again. For a moment Clarice fancied that the gates must be shut, but as she bent forward and looked across Drake, she saw that they were open. She turned her eyes to her companion. He was sitting bolt upright with an unfamiliar expression of irresolution upon his face, and he was doubtfully drawing the lash of the whip to and fro across the horse's back.

Clarice felt that her life was in the balance. 'Yes,' she whispered.

'No!' Drake almost shouted the word. He turned the horse through the gates and drove in a gallop to the door of the house. Clarice heard him draw a deep breath of relief as he jumped to the ground. As he was pulling off his gloves in the hall, Clarice brushed past him and ran quickly up the stairs. He was roused from his reverie by the arrival of the rest of the party.

Clarice sent word downstairs that she was tired and would not appear at supper.

But an hour later Sidney Mallinson found her seated by the open window. She had not even taken off her hat or gloves. Once or twice he seemed on the point of speaking, but she faced him steadily and her manner even invited his questions. Mallinson turned away with the questions unasked. But he lay long awake that night, thinking; and his resentment against Drake gained new fuel from his thoughts.

The frankness of his wife's admiration for Drake had before this awakened his suspicions, and the suspicions had become certain knowledge. He guessed, too, that to some degree Drake returned his wife's inclination, and he began immediately on that account to set a higher value upon the possession of her than he had lately done.

Once Clarice heard him laugh aloud harshly. He was thinking of the relationship in which he had set Drake to himself in that first novel which he had written. Actually the relationship was reversed. 'No, not yet,' he said to himself. But it would be, unless he could hit upon some plan. The day was breaking when his plan came to him.

CHAPTER XV

The next morning Drake's seat at the breakfast table was empty.

'He caught the early train from Bentbridge,' Captain Le Mesurier explained. 'Business, I suppose. He told me last thing yesterday night that he had to go.'

Clarice coloured and lowered her eyes to her plate. Mallinson noticed her embarrassment, and took it for evidence of some secret understanding between her and Drake. He became yet more firmly resolved to put his idea into action.

'You are not in a hurry,' said Captain Le Mesurier. 'You had better stay the week out.'

Mallinson saw his wife raise her head quickly as though she was about to object, and immediately accepted the invitation. Parliament would not meet for three weeks, he reckoned, since there were still the county members to be elected.

Clarice spent the week in defining the relationship in which she and Drake were henceforth to stand towards each other. They were to be animated by a stern spirit of duty,—by the same spirit, in fact, which had compelled Drake to court-martial Gorley in Africa, and subsequently to detail the episode to her. Duty was to keep them apart. She came to think of duty as a row of footlights across which they could from time to time look into each other's eyes.

Clarice felt that there was something very reassuring and protective in this notion of duty. It justified her in buying a copy of *Frou-Frou*, which lay upon the bookstall at Bentbridge railway station, and in studying it continuously all the way from Bentbridge to London. She was impelled to purchase it by a recollection that Drake had first been introduced to her at a performance of that play, and his criticisms returned to her thoughts as she read the dialogue. The play had seemed true to him, the disaster inevitable— given the particular characters, and she bore the qualification particularly in mind. There was a difference between *Frou-Frou* and a woman animated by a sense of duty; a difference of kind, rather than of degree. Sidney Mallinson remarked the book which she was reading, but he made no comment whatsoever.

The next morning he paid a long call upon the editor of the *Meteor*.

Meanwhile, Drake was devoting himself to the business of the Matanga Company, with an assiduity unusual even for him. Fielding discovered that he seldom left the city before ten at night, and felt it incumbent to expostulate with him. 'You can't go on like this for much longer, you know. You had better take a rest. There's no need for all this work.'

'There is,' replied Drake. 'I want to clear off arrears, because I am not sure that I oughtn't to go out again to Matanga. You see I can do it quite easily. Parliament meets in a fortnight to vote supplies. It will adjourn, it's thought, three weeks later. I could leave England in September, and get back easily in time for the regular sessions.'

'But why should you go at all?' asked Fielding. 'You haven't been back a year as it is.'

'I know,' said Drake slowly. 'But it seems to me that it would inspire confidence, and that sort of thing, if one of us were out there as much as possible. You see, thanks to you and Burl, I can leave everything here quite safely,' and he returned to his desk as though the discussion was ended.

A week later he received an invitation to dinner from Mr. Le Mesurier, and the invitation was so worded that he could find no becoming excuse to decline it. The dinner was given, the note stated, in order to celebrate his victory at Bentbridge. Fielding and he went together, and when they arrived, they found Mallinson taking off his coat in the hall.

'Where have you been all this time?' asked Fielding. 'I haven't seen you about.'

'At Clapham,' replied Mallinson.

'I don't know it.'

'It's a suburb to the south-west.'

'That's why.'

'My mother lives there.'

'I am very sorry.'

The words might have been intended to convey either an apology, or an expression of sympathy with his mother. Mallinson preferred to take them in the former sense. 'I took my wife down there,' he continued. 'She wanted more quiet than one can get in London.'

Fielding noticed, however, that Clapham quiet had not materially benefited Mrs. Mallinson. He commented on her worn appearance to Mrs. Willoughby, when they were seated at the dinner-table.

'She has been staying, she tells me, with her husband's people,' replied Mrs. Willoughby. 'I fancy she finds them trying.'

Clarice was placed next to Drake, upon the opposite side to Mrs. Willoughby, and out of ear-shot, and was endeavouring to talk to him indifferently. 'You never take a holiday, I suppose. Where are you going this year?' she asked.

'To Matanga,' said Drake.

'Matanga! Oh no.' The words slipped from her lips before she was able to check them.

'I think that my place is there,' returned Drake, 'at all events for the moment. I shall go as soon as the House rises.'

'I thought you didn't mean to leave London again.'

'One gets over ideas of that kind. After all, my interests lie in Matanga, and one gets a kind of affection for the place which makes your fortune.'

The recantation was uttered with sufficient awkwardness. But Clarice was too engrossed in her own thoughts to notice his embarrassment. 'Do you remember when I first met you?' she asked. 'It was at a performance of *Frou-Frou*.'

'I remember quite well,' said he. 'I was rather struck with the play.'

'I have been reading it lately.'

Drake started at the significant tone in which the words were spoken. 'Really?' he said, with an uneasy laugh. 'What impressed me was that scene at Venice, where Gilberte and De Valreas read over the list of plays in the Paris newspapers, and realise what they have thrown away, and for how little. It seemed to me the saddest scene I had ever witnessed.'

'Yes,' interposed Clarice quickly. 'But because Paris and its theatres meant so much to them. I remember what you said, that everything in the play seemed so true just to those characters, Gilberte and De Valreas.'

She glanced at him as she uttered the last name. Drake understood that she was drawing a distinction between him and the fashionable lounger of the play.

'Besides,' she went on, dropping her voice, 'Gilberte left a child behind her. Her unhappiness turned on that.'

'In a way, no doubt, but the loss of friends, station, home, counts for something—for enough to destroy her liking for De Valreas at all events.'

'For De Valreas!' insisted Clarice. 'He was not worth the sacrifice.' She paused for a moment, and then continued diffidently. 'There's something else; I hardly like to tell you it. You wouldn't notice it from seeing the play. I didn't; but it came to me when I read the book. I think the play's absolutely untrue, yes, even to those characters, in one respect.'

'And what's that?' asked Drake.

Clarice glanced round. Her neighbours, she perceived, were talking. Mrs. Willoughby was too far off to hear. She dropped her voice to a yet lower key and said, 'They make the husband kill the lover in the duel. It's always the end in books and plays; but really the opposite of that would happen.'

Drake leant back in his chair and stared at her. 'What do you mean?'

'Hush!' she said warningly, and turning away she spoke for a little to the man on the other side of her. Then she turned back. 'I mean,' she said, 'if two people really care for one another, their love would triumph over everything—everything. De Valreas would have killed the husband.' She spoke with an intense conviction of the truth of what she said.

'But, my dear child!' replied Drake. 'You—oh, you don't really believe that.'

'I do,' she answered. 'You see, there are so few people who really care for one another. If you find two who do, I am sure they would conquer, whatever stood in the way.'

The conversation was interrupted, to Drake's relief, by Captain Le Mesurier. He rose from the corner of the table to propose the health of the guest of the evening. He said that he was proud to be represented in Parliament by a man of Stephen Drake's calibre. If there was anything of which he was prouder, it was the way in which the election had been fought at Bentbridge. That election was the triumph not merely of a man or a cause, but of a method; and that method was honesty and fair-play. 'We never indulged in personalities,' he continued, with shameless sincerity. 'I have

A. E. W. Mason

always myself been very strong on that point. Fight of course for all you're worth, but never indulge in personalities. It's a good rule. It's a rule that helped Stephen Drake to win his seat. We followed it. We left the lies for the opponent to tell, and he told them. But we never did and never will indulge in contemptible personalities.'

The Captain subsided to a gentle rapping of forks and spoons upon the table, while Fielding said pointedly, 'Yes, Captain, you deserve your holidays,' and he emphasised the word. The Captain caught the allusion and laughed heartily. It was evident that he saw no inconsistency between the epigram and his professed method of contesting an election.

Drake replied shortly, and the ladies retired. Mallinson moved round the table, and seated himself in the chair which Clarice had left.

'Do you think of speaking at all during this session?' he asked.

'I am not quite sure,' replied Drake; 'but I rather think I shall on the colonial vote. You see there's first-class wheat-growing land in Africa, quite near to the west coast. We import practically all that we use in England. Well, why shouldn't we import it from our own dominions? Besides, the route would be so much safer in times of war, unless, of course, we were at war with France. Ships could slip up the coast of Africa, across the bay and into Plymouth with much less risk than if they have to sail from the Argentines or some place like that. I believe, if the Colonial Office could be induced to move in the matter, the idea might be carried out. What do you think?'

Mallinson carelessly assented and returned to his seat.

For the remainder of the evening Drake avoided Clarice. As he was taking his leave, however, she came up to him. He shook her by the hand and she whispered one word to him, 'Matanga.' Drake could not mistake the note of longing in her voice, and as he drove to his chambers the temptation with which he had wrestled at the gates of Garples assailed him again, and with double force. He had but to speak, he knew, and she would come. The loneliness of his rooms made the struggle yet harder, yet more doubtful. He pictured to himself what he had never had, a home, and he located that home in Matanga. The arid plain blossomed in his imagination, for he saw the weariness die out of Clarice's face.

He tossed restlessly through the night, until one thought emerged from the turmoil of his ideas, fashioned itself into a fact, and stood framed there before his eyes. He held the future of Clarice in the hollow of his hand. Her fate rested upon his decision, and he must decide.

Drake rose and walked out on to the balcony, as the dawn was breaking over London. A white mist was crawling above the Thames; he could see a glimpse of the water here and there as the mist shredded. He turned to the west and looked towards Westminster, recollecting how his name and purposes had centred there as though drawn by a magnet. But in that clear morning light they seemed unreal and purposeless. One immediate responsibility invaded him, and, contrasted with that, his ambitions dwindled into vanities. He filled no place, he realised, which would be vacant unless he occupied it. He had to decide for Clarice and solely for her.

Drake took up his hat and walked out of London to Elm Tree Hill. There, gazing down upon its spires asparkle in the early sunlight, while the city gradually awoke and the hum of its stirring began to swell through the air, he came to his decision. Clarice belonged to London; he did not. In

Matanga she would be content—for how long? The roughness, the absence of her kind and class, the makeshift air of transition, would soon destroy its charm of novelty. Every instinct would draw her back to London, and the way would be barred, whilst for him Matanga was a province in which every capacity he possessed could find employment and exercise. He would leave England for Matanga when this short session was over; he would resign his seat and settle there for good. For if he stayed in London, every step which he took, every advance which he made, would only add to Clarice's miseries.

Thus he decided, and walked back with his mind at rest, without regret for the loss of his ambitions, without, indeed, any real consciousness of the sacrifice which he had it in his thoughts to make.

Thus he decided, but as he left his office on the afternoon of the day whereon he was to make his speech in the House of Commons, Fielding rushed up to him with a copy of the *Meteor*.

'Look!' he said, and pointed to an article. Drake took the paper and read the article through. His face darkened as he read. The article had a headline which puzzled Drake for a moment. It was entitled *The Drabious Duke*, and it proceeded to set out the episode of Gorley's court-martial and execution. The facts, Drake recognised, were not exaggerated, but the sting lay in the suggestion with which it concluded.

'We have no doubt,' the leader-writer stated, 'that both the court-martial and execution were in accordance with the letter of the law, but, since Mr. Stephen Drake is now one of the legislators of this country, we feel it our duty to submit two facts for the consideration of our readers. In the first place we would call attention to the secrecy in which the incident has been carefully shrouded. In the second, Gorley undoubtedly secured a considerable quantity of gold-dust. Now, it is perfectly well known that the Government of Matanga pays a commission on all gold-dust brought down to the coast. We have gone into the matter carefully, and we positively assert that no commission whatever was paid in any such plunder during the two months which followed Mr. Drake's return from Boruwimi. What, then, became of it? We ask our readers to weigh these two facts dispassionately, and we feel justified in adding that Mr. Drake would have been quite within his rights in showing clemency to Gorley, or in bringing him back to undergo a regular trial. However, he preferred to execute him on the spot.'

'He makes me out a thief and a murderer,' said Drake. 'I wonder where he got the story from?'

Fielding answered slowly, 'I am afraid that I can throw some light on that. I told Mallinson some time ago, before he was married.'

'Mallinson!' exclaimed Drake, stopping in the street. 'Oh, you think the article comes from him?' Then he turned to Fielding. 'And how did you know of it?'

'Well,' said Fielding with some hesitation, 'Mrs. Willoughby told me.'

'Why?'

'We neither of us, of course, knew you very well then. Mrs. Willoughby had only just met you, and she didn't feel quite certain that Clarice ought to be kept in ignorance of the matter, so she asked my advice.'

A. E. W. Mason

'Quite so,' answered Drake. 'I understand. You thought Clarice ought to be informed, and you were right. I told her of the matter myself.'

'No,' exclaimed Fielding; 'I'll tell you the whole truth while I am about it. I advised Mrs. Willoughby to say nothing, but I behaved like a damned cad, and told Mallinson myself afterwards. I had quite another reason for telling him.'

'Oh, never mind!' broke in Drake. 'The question is, what's to be done now?'

'You must sue the paper!'

'Of course. I was thinking whether I couldn't mention the matter to-night in the House of Commons. You see it has got into the papers that I mean to speak, and perhaps I ought to make use of the opportunity.'

Fielding jumped at the idea. 'By Jove, yes,' he said. 'I should think, in fact, the directors of the Company will rather expect it.'

They walked together until they reached the corner of Parliament Street; there they stopped.

'I am awfully sorry, Drake,' said Fielding. 'I behaved like a blackguard.'

Drake again cut him short. 'Oh, I don't see that. The thing looked fishy, I don't doubt, and you weren't bound to me in any way. Good-bye,' and he held out his hand with a cordial smile.

'Good-bye,' said Fielding, and they separated.

On reaching his flat Drake was informed that a lady was waiting to see him. He crossed the passage and opened the door of his sitting-room. Mrs. Mallinson was standing by the window.

A. E. W. Mason

CHAPTER XVI

She turned quickly as the door closed and took a step towards the centre of the room. Drake perceived that she had a copy of the *Meteor* in her hand. 'You have seen this?' she asked.

'Yes.' He remained by the door with his hand on the knob.

'And you guessed who wrote it?'

'I have been told.' He answered her coldly and quietly.

'I know what you think,' she replied. 'But it's not true. I never told him the story. He knew it long ago—before you went back to Matanga—before I married him.' Her voice took a pleading tone. 'You will believe that, won't you?'

'It never occurred to me that you had told him. I know, in fact, who did. But even if you had—well, you had the right to tell him.' Clarice gave a stamp of impatience. 'He is your husband.'

'My husband!' she interrupted, and she tore the newspaper across and dropped it on to the floor. 'My husband! Ah, I wouldn't have believed that even he could have done a thing so mean. And, to add to the meanness of it, he went away yesterday, for a week. I know why, now; he dared not face me.' Then of a sudden her voice softened. 'But it's my fault too, in a way,' she went on. 'He knew the story a long time ago, and never used it. I don't suppose he would have used it now, if I hadn't—since your election—let him see—' She broke off the sentence, and took a step nearer to Drake. 'Stephen, I meant to let him see.'

Drake drew himself up against the door. It would be no longer of any service to her, he thought, if he left England and returned to Matanga. Something more trenchant was needed.

He reflected again that he filled no place which another could not fill, and the reflection took a wider meaning than it had done before. 'Yes,' he said; 'it's very awkward that it should all come out just now.'

Clarice stared at him in perplexity. 'Awkward that it should all come out,' she repeated vaguely; and then, with an accent of relief, 'You mean that it will injure the Company?'

'Not so much that. The Company can run without me—quite well now—I am certain of it.' He spoke as though he was endeavouring to assure himself of what he said.

'But it won't hurt you, really,' she exclaimed. 'You can disprove the charges, and of course you must, I know you hesitate—for my sake—to bring an action and expose the writer. But you must, and I don't think,' she lowered her eyes to the ground, 'you would hurt me by doing that.' For a moment she was silent. Drake made no answer, and she raised her eyes again to his face. 'You can disprove it—oh, of course,' she said, with a little anxious laugh.

'That depends,' he answered slowly, 'upon how much the

A. E. W. Mason

Meteor knows.'

Clarice drew back and caught at the table to steady herself. Once or twice she pressed her hand across her forehead. 'Oh, don't stand like that,' she burst out, 'as if it was all true.'

'But they can't prove it's true,' exclaimed Drake, with a trace of cunning in his voice. 'No; they can't prove it's true.'

'But is it?' Clarice stood in front of him, her hands clenched. Drake dropped his eyes from her face, raised them again, and again lowered them. 'Is it?' she repeated, and her voice rose to the tone of a demand.

'Yes,' and he answered her in a whisper.

Clarice recoiled from him with a cry of disgust. She noticed that he drew a long breath—of relief, it seemed—like the criminal when his crime is at last brought home to him. 'Then all that story,' she began, 'you told me at Beaufort Gardens about—about Boruwimi was just meant to deceive me. You talked about duty! Duty compelled you! You would have hanged Gorley just the same had you known that he had been engaged to me.' She began to laugh hysterically. 'It was all duty,—duty from beginning to end, and I believed you. Heaven help me, I came to honour you for it. And in reality it was a lie!' She lashed the words at him, but he stood patiently, and made no rejoinder. 'I always wondered why you told me the story,' she continued. 'You felt that I had a right to know, I remember. And you felt bound to tell me. It's clear enough now why you felt bound. You had found out, I suppose, that my husband knew—' She stopped suddenly, as though some new thought had flashed into her mind. 'And I came here to give up everything—just for your sake. Oh, suppose that I hadn't found you out!'

She stooped and picked up from the floor the torn pages of the *Meteor*. She folded them carefully and then moved towards the door. Drake opened it and stood aside.

Clarice went out, called a hansom and drove home. When she arrived there she ordered tea to be brought to the drawing-room and sat down and again read the article in the *Meteor*. When the tea was brought, she ordered it to be taken into Sidney's study. She walked restlessly about that room, as though she was trying to habituate herself to it. A green shade lay upon the writing-table, which her husband was accustomed to wear over his eyes. She took it up, looked at it for a little, and then threw it down again with an air of weariness and distaste. A few minutes later Percy Conway called and was admitted.

CHAPTER XVII

Fielding opened his newspaper the next morning with
unusual eagerness, and, turning to the Parliamentary reports,
glanced down column after column in search of Drake's
speech. The absence of it threw him into some consternation.
He tossed the newspaper on to the breakfast-table and rose
from his seat. As he moved, however, he caught sight of
Drake's name at the beginning of a leader, and he read the
leader through. It dealt with the accusation of the *Meteor*,
and expressed considerable surprise that Drake had not
seized the opportunity of denying it in the House of
Commons. It was mentioned that Drake had not been seen
there at any time during the course of the evening.

Fielding jumped to the conclusion that he had met with an
accident, and set out for his chambers on the instant. He found
Drake quietly eating his breakfast. Only half the table,
however, was laid for the meal; the other half was littered with
papers and correspondence, while a pile of stamped letters
stood on one corner. 'I was expecting you,' said Drake quietly.

'Why, what on earth has happened?' asked Fielding. 'Why
didn't you speak last night?'

'I thought it would be the wisest plan to leave the matter
alone.'

'But you can't,' exclaimed Fielding. 'Read this!' and he handed to him the newspaper. 'You can't leave it alone.'

'I can, and shall,' replied Drake, and he returned to his breakfast.

'But, my dear fellow, you can't understand what that means! Read the leader, then.' Drake glanced quickly down it. 'Now, do you understand? It means utter ruin, utter disgrace, unless you answer this charge, and answer it at once. You will have created a false enough impression already.' Drake, however, made no response beyond a shrug of his shoulders. 'But, good Lord, man,' continued Fielding, 'your name's at stake. You can't sit quiet as if this was an irresponsible piece of paragraph-writing. You would have to resign your seat in Parliament, your connection with the Matanga Company—everything. You couldn't possibly live in England.'

'Do you think I haven't counted up precisely what inaction is going to cost me?' interrupted Drake. 'Look here!' and he took a couple of letters from the pile and handed them to Fielding. One was addressed to the whip of his party, and the other to the directors of the Matanga Concessions. 'And I leave Charing Cross at ten o'clock this morning.'

Fielding looked at his watch; it was half-past nine. 'Then you mean to run away?' he gasped. 'But, in Heaven's name, why?'

'For an obvious reason. Yesterday I believed that I could meet the charge. But something has happened since then, and I know now that I can't.'

Fielding started back. 'Do you mean to tell me, as man to man, that the accusation's true.'

'As man to man,' repeated Drake steadily, 'I tell you that it

A. E. W. Mason

is true.'

Fielding stared at him for a minute. Then he said, 'Drake, you're a damned liar.'

'We haven't much time,' said Drake, 'and I would like to say something to you about the future of the Matanga settlement. You will take my place, I suppose. You can, and ought to'; and he entered at once into details on administration.

The advice, however, was lost upon Fielding. Once he interrupted Drake. 'How many white men were with you on the Boruwimi expedition?' he asked.

'Four,' answered Drake, and he gave the names. 'They are dead, though. Two died of fever on the way back; one was killed in a subsequent expedition, and the fourth was drowned about eighteen months ago off Walfisch Bay.' A noise of portmanteaux being dragged along the passage penetrated through the closed door. Drake looked at his watch, and started to his feet. 'I must be off,' he said; 'I am late as it is. You might do something for me, and that is to post these letters.'

'But, man, you are not really going?'

Drake for answer put on his hat and took up his stick. 'Good-bye,' he said.

'But, look here! Do you ask me to believe that you would have been giving me all this advice, if you had really done what that infernal paper makes you out to have done?'

'I'll give you a final piece of advice too. Give up philandering and get married!'

With that he opened the door and went out, and a few seconds later Fielding heard the sound of his cab-wheels rattle on the pavement.

Drake, on reaching Charing Cross, found that he had more time to spare than he had reckoned. He was walking slowly along the train in search of an empty compartment when, from a window a few paces ahead of him, a face flashed out, and as suddenly withdrew. The face was Conway's, and Drake felt that the sudden withdrawal meant a distinct desire to avoid recognition. He set the desire down to the unrepulsed attack of the *Meteor*, and since he had no inclination to force his company upon Conway, he turned on his heel and moved towards the other end of the train. He was just opposite the archway of the booking-office when a woman, heavily veiled and of a slight figure, came out of it. At the sight of Drake she came to a dead stop, and so attracted his attention. Then she quickly turned her back to him, walked to the bookstall, and slipped round the side of it into the waiting-room. Drake wheeled about again. Conway's head was stretched out of the window; and he was gazing towards the bookstall.

Drake was in no doubt as to who the woman was, and he felt his heart turn to stone. He walked quickly back until he reached Conway's compartment. It was empty save for him, but there was a reserved label in the window.

'Holloa!' said Conway, awkwardly enough. 'Are you going by this train? You had better find a seat if you are.'

'But I'm not,' said Drake; 'I thought of going, but I have changed my mind.' He leaned against the door of the carriage chatting incessantly to Conway, with an eye upon the waiting-room. Once he saw the woman appear at the door, but she retired again. Meanwhile Conway's embarrassment

A. E. W. Mason

increased. He said 'Good-bye' to Drake at least half-a-dozen times, but on each occasion Drake had something new to say to him. At last the whistle sounded and the train began to move. 'I say,' cried Drake, running along by the carriage. 'My luggage is in the van. You might bring it back with you from Dover, if you will,' and he stood watching the train until it disappeared under the shed.

Then he walked into the waiting-room. He saw Clarice seated in a corner, and went straight to her. She noticed that his face was white and set, and she rose with some instinct of defiance. 'I owe you an apology,' he said abruptly. 'The *Meteor* is untrue from the first word to the last. I mean to stay in London, and fight it; yesterday afternoon I told you lies.'

'Why?' she asked.

'Sheer lunacy,' said he; and he got into a cab and drove to the offices of his solicitor.

CHAPTER XVIII

Meanwhile Fielding picked up the pile of letters from the table in Drake's chambers and went down into the street. He paused for a moment or two at the pillar-box weighing the letters in his hand. Then he slipped them into his pocket and hurried to Mrs. Willoughby's.

Mrs. Willoughby was moving restlessly about the drawing-room as he was shown in. She turned impulsively towards him, holding out both hands. 'I so hoped you would come,' she said. 'Well? You have seen him?'

'Yes.'

'What does he mean to do?' she asked anxiously, taking from a chair a copy of the *Meteor*.

'Nothing,' replied Fielding. 'He resigns his seat; he gives up his directorship; he is leaving England.'

Mrs. Willoughby's first look was of sheer incredulity. 'It's impossible!' she exclaimed.

'I have just returned from his chambers. He has started from Charing Cross already.'

Mrs. Willoughby sat down in the window-seat, and her look of incredulity gradually changed to one of comprehension. 'And he took such delight in London,' she said, with a break in her voice; 'just like a schoolboy.'

Fielding nodded gloomily. 'I did my best to dissuade him,' he said. 'I practically told him he was a coward to run away. But you know the man. He had made up his mind not to face the charge. And yet I can't believe it's true.'

'Believe it!' exclaimed Mrs. Willoughby, with a hint of something dangerously near to scorn in her voice.

'I know, I know,' answered Fielding. 'Still Drake pleads guilty. He sacrifices everything, an established position, unusual prospects—everything, by pleading guilty. You see, that's the point. He has every imaginable inducement to make him face the accusation, even if he has only the merest chance of winning, and yet he runs away. He runs away— Drake does. There's only one inference—'

'For the world to draw,' interrupted Mrs. Willoughby; 'and doubtless he meant the world to draw it. But you and I should know him better.'

'Yes,' Fielding admitted, 'Yes.' He began to walk about the room. 'But what's the reason? Drake's action, if this statement is a libel, is the action of a madman.'

'A madman? Yes! Don Quixote was mad even in his century,' replied Mrs. Willoughby. 'I can give you the reason. Clarice was with him yesterday afternoon.'

'Yesterday?' said Fielding. 'Why, I walked home with Drake from the City myself.'

'But you didn't go in with him.'

'No; I left him alone to arrange his speech. He meant to mention this very charge.'

Mrs. Willoughby started to her feet. 'Then that settles it,' she said. 'Clarice was waiting for him in his rooms. Oh, if you had only gone in with him! You remember what I wrote to you, that he would lie in the mud if he thought it would save her. Well, that is what he has done. Clarice came here this very morning and told me what had happened. She went to his chambers, determined never to return to her husband, prepared to sacrifice—I give you her words, not mine—to sacrifice herself, her name, and for his sake. But when she showed him the *Meteor* her suspicions were aroused by his manner, and she forced the truth out of him.'

Fielding gave a short, contemptuous laugh. 'Forced the truth out of him! She actually told you that?'

'And what's more, she believes it. Oh the waste, the waste of a man like that upon a doll like her. I suppose there's nothing to be done?'

'Nothing; if he won't defend himself, our defence won't carry any weight,' he went on, with a change of tone. 'But I don't see what real good he does, even to her. She goes back to her husband now, but next month or next year there'll be somebody else.'

'Yes,' replied Mrs. Willoughby; 'but I hardly fancy Stephen Drake would consider that. I believe he would feel that he had no right to speculate on what may not happen. He would just see this one clear, definite, immediate thing to do, and simply do it.' She spoke the sentence with a slow emphasis upon each word, and Fielding moved uneasily. It seemed to

A. E. W. Mason

strike an accusation at him. He braced himself to make the same confession to Mrs. Willoughby which he had made that afternoon before to Drake. But, before he could speak it, Mrs. Willoughby put to him a question. 'Tell me, did he seem to mind much?'

'No,' Fielding answered with an air of relief. His confession was deferred, if only for a minute. 'He seemed cheerful enough. The last thing he did,' and he paused for a second, 'was to give me advice about the management of the Matanga Company.'

'That's so like him,' she said gently. Then she looked up with a start of interest. 'You are going to take his place?' she asked.

'He said I ought to. I know more about it than the other directors. Of course they mayn't appoint me, but I expect they will.' Mrs. Willoughby was silent. She moved away from the window and stood by the fireplace. Fielding crossed to her. 'Drake gave me one other piece of advice,' he said hesitatingly,—'not about business. It concerned me and just one other person.' He pitched the remark in an interrogative key.

Mrs. Willoughby glanced quickly towards him with just the hint of a smile dimpling about the corners of her lips. Fielding found it very difficult to go on, but there was one clear, definite, immediate thing for him to do as well, he said. 'Before I act on it there is something I ought to tell you.' He paused for a second, and the trouble in his voice perplexed Mrs. Willoughby. 'Whom do you think Mallinson got his knowledge about Gorley from?'

Mrs. Willoughby took a step forward. 'Whom? Why,' and she gave a little anxious laugh, 'from Clarice, of course.'

'No.'

Mrs. Willoughby looked at him for a moment in silence. Then she drew back again. 'You told him?' she asked with a quiet wonder. 'Yes,' Fielding nodded. 'But I only told you,' she said, 'because I wanted your advice. What made you tell him? There must have been some reason, some good reason, some necessity.'

'No; there was no necessity, no good reason, no reason at all,' Fielding replied doggedly. 'I told him because—' he stopped abruptly; the reason seemed too pitiful for him even to relate.

'Well, because?' asked Mrs. Willoughby. There was a note of hardness in the utterance. Fielding raised his eyes and glanced at her face. 'It comes too late,' he said unconsciously, and he was thinking of Drake's advice.

'The reason!' she insisted, taking no notice of the sentence. 'The reason!'

'I told Mallinson at the time when I was always meeting him here.'

Mrs. Willoughby gave a start. 'And because of that?' she cried.

'Yes,' said he. 'I thought the knowledge might give him a fairer,' he changed the word, 'a better, chance with Clarice.'

'Oh, how mean!' exclaimed Mrs. Willoughby, not so much in anger as in absolute disappointment. She turned away from him, and stood for a little looking out of the window. Then she said, 'Good-bye.'

And Fielding took his hat and left the house. He went down

to the office, and was told that Drake wanted to see him.

'Drake!' he exclaimed. He pushed open the door of Drake's private office, and the latter looked up from his papers.

'You called me a damned liar this morning,' he said, 'and you were right.'

Fielding dropped into a chair. 'What do you mean?'

'That there's not a word of truth in the *Meteor's* charges, and I am prosecuting the editor. Did you post those letters?'

Fielding pulled them out of his pocket and threw them on to the table. 'Thanks,' said Drake, 'that's fortunate.'

Fielding did not inquire into the cause of Drake's change of purpose, and it was some while before he understood it. For Mrs. Willoughby held no further discussions with him in the drawing-room at Knightsbridge.

THE END

ABOUT THE AUTHOR

Alfred Edward Woodley Mason (7 May 1865 Dulwich, London - 22 November 1948 London) was a British author.

He studied at Dulwich College and graduated from Trinity College, Oxford in 1888.

His first novel, A Romance of Wastdale, was published in 1895. He is the author of more than twenty books, among them The Four Feathers, originally published in London in 1902. His next successful work was At The Villa Rose (1910), where he introduced his French detective, Hanaud.

Mason was elected as a Liberal Member of Parliament for Coventry in the 1906 general election. He served only a single term in Parliament, retiring at the next general election in January 1910.

Mason rose to the rank of major during the First World War serving with The Manchester Regiment and the Royal Marine Light Infantry. His military career included work in naval intelligence, serving in Spain and Mexico, where he set up counter-espionage networks on behalf of the British government.

He died in 1948 while working on a non-fiction book about Admiral Robert Blake.

Choose from Thousands of 1stWorldLibrary Classics By

A. M. Barnard
Ada Leverson
Adolphus William Ward
Aesop
Agatha Christie
Alexander Aaronsohn
Alexander Kielland
Alexandre Dumas
Alfred Gatty
Alfred Ollivant
Alice Duer Miller
Alice Turner Curtis
Alice Dunbar
Allen Chapman
Alleyne Ireland
Ambrose Bierce
Amelia E. Barr
Amory H. Bradford
Andrew Lang
Andrew McFarland Davis
Andy Adams
Angela Brazil
Anna Alice Chapin
Anna Sewell
Annie Besant
Annie Hamilton Donnell
Annie Payson Call
Annie Roe Carr
Annonaymous
Anton Chekhov
Archibald Lee Fletcher
Arnold Bennett
Arthur C. Benson
Arthur Conan Doyle
Arthur M. Winfield
Arthur Ransome
Arthur Schnitzler
Arthur Train
Atticus
B.H. Baden-Powell
B. M. Bower
B. C. Chatterjee
Baroness Emmuska Orczy
Baroness Orczy
Basil King
Bayard Taylor
Ben Macomber
Bertha Muzzy Bower
Bjornstjerne Bjornson

Booth Tarkington
Boyd Cable
Bram Stoker
C. Collodi
C. E. Orr
C. M. Ingleby
Carolyn Wells
Catherine Parr Traill
Charles A. Eastman
Charles Amory Beach
Charles Dickens
Charles Dudley Warner
Charles Farrar Browne
Charles Ives
Charles Kingsley
Charles Klein
Charles Hanson Towne
Charles Lathrop Pack
Charles Romyn Dake
Charles Whibley
Charles Willing Beale
Charlotte M. Braeme
Charlotte M. Yonge
Charlotte Perkins Stetson
Clair W. Hayes
Clarence Day Jr.
Clarence E. Mulford
Clemence Housman
Confucius
Coningsby Dawson
Cornelis DeWitt Wilcox
Cyril Burleigh
D. H. Lawrence
Daniel Defoe
David Garnett
Dinah Craik
Don Carlos Janes
Donald Keyhoe
Dorothy Kilner
Dougan Clark
Douglas Fairbanks
E. Nesbit
E. P. Roe
E. Phillips Oppenheim
E. S. Brooks
Earl Barnes
Edgar Rice Burroughs
Edith Van Dyne
Edith Wharton

Edward Everett Hale
Edward J. O'Biren
Edward S. Ellis
Edwin L. Arnold
Eleanor Atkins
Eleanor Hallowell Abbott
Eliot Gregory
Elizabeth Gaskell
Elizabeth McCracken
Elizabeth Von Arnim
Ellem Key
Emerson Hough
Emilie F. Carlen
Emily Bronte
Emily Dickinson
Enid Bagnold
Enilor Macartney Lane
Erasmus W. Jones
Ernie Howard Pie
Ethel May Dell
Ethel Turner
Ethel Watts Mumford
Eugene Sue
Eugenie Foa
Eugene Wood
Eustace Hale Ball
Evelyn Everett-green
Everard Cotes
F. H. Cheley
F. J. Cross
F. Marion Crawford
Fannie E. Newberry
Federick Austin Ogg
Ferdinand Ossendowski
Fergus Hume
Florence A. Kilpatrick
Fremont B. Deering
Francis Bacon
Francis Darwin
Frances Hodgson Burnett
Frances Parkinson Keyes
Frank Gee Patchin
Frank Harris
Frank Jewett Mather
Frank L. Packard
Frank V. Webster
Frederic Stewart Isham
Frederick Trevor Hill
Frederick Winslow Taylor

Friedrich Kerst
Friedrich Nietzsche
Fyodor Dostoyevsky
G.A. Henty
G.K. Chesterton
Gabrielle E. Jackson
Garrett P. Serviss
Gaston Leroux
George A. Warren
George Ade
Geroge Bernard Shaw
George Cary Eggleston
George Durston
George Ebers
George Eliot
George Gissing
George MacDonald
George Meredith
George Orwell
George Sylvester Viereck
George Tucker
George W. Cable
George Wharton James
Gertrude Atherton
Gordon Casserly
Grace E. King
Grace Gallatin
Grace Greenwood
Grant Allen
Guillermo A. Sherwell
Gulielma Zollinger
Gustav Flaubert
H. A. Cody
H. B. Irving
H.C. Bailey
H. G. Wells
H. H. Munro
H. Irving Hancock
H. R. Naylor
H. Rider Haggard
H. W. C. Davis
Haldeman Julius
Hall Caine
Hamilton Wright Mabie
Hans Christian Andersen
Harold Avery
Harold McGrath
Harriet Beecher Stowe
Harry Castlemon
Harry Coghill
Harry Houidini

Hayden Carruth
Helent Hunt Jackson
Helen Nicolay
Hendrik Conscience
Hendy David Thoreau
Henri Barbusse
Henrik Ibsen
Henry Adams
Henry Ford
Henry Frost
Henry James
Henry Jones Ford
Henry Seton Merriman
Henry W Longfellow
Herbert A. Giles
Herbert Carter
Herbert N. Casson
Herman Hesse
Hildegard G. Frey
Homer
Honore De Balzac
Horace B. Day
Horace Walpole
Horatio Alger Jr.
Howard Pyle
Howard R. Garis
Hugh Lofting
Hugh Walpole
Humphry Ward
Ian Maclaren
Inez Haynes Gillmore
Irving Bacheller
Isabel Cecilia Williams
Isabel Hornibrook
Israel Abrahams
Ivan Turgenev
J.G.Austin
J. Henri Fabre
J. M. Barrie
J. M. Walsh
J. Macdonald Oxley
J. R. Miller
J. S. Fletcher
J. S. Knowles
J. Storer Clouston
J. W. Duffield
Jack London
Jacob Abbott
James Allen
James Andrews
James Baldwin

James Branch Cabell
James DeMille
James Joyce
James Lane Allen
James Lane Allen
James Oliver Curwood
James Oppenheim
James Otis
James R. Driscoll
Jane Abbott
Jane Austen
Jane L. Stewart
Janet Aldridge
Jens Peter Jacobsen
Jerome K. Jerome
Jessie Graham Flower
John Buchan
John Burroughs
John Cournos
John F. Kennedy
John Gay
John Glasworthy
John Habberton
John Joy Bell
John Kendrick Bangs
John Milton
John Philip Sousa
John Taintor Foote
Jonas Lauritz Idemil Lie
Jonathan Swift
Joseph A. Altsheler
Joseph Carey
Joseph Conrad
Joseph E. Badger Jr
Joseph Hergesheimer
Joseph Jacobs
Jules Vernes
Julian Hawthrone
Julie A Lippmann
Justin Huntly McCarthy
Kakuzo Okakura
Karle Wilson Baker
Kate Chopin
Kenneth Grahame
Kenneth McGaffey
Kate Langley Bosher
Kate Langley Bosher
Katherine Cecil Thurston
Katherine Stokes
L. A. Abbot
L. T. Meade

L. Frank Baum
Latta Griswold
Laura Dent Crane
Laura Lee Hope
Laurence Housman
Lawrence Beasley
Leo Tolstoy
Leonid Andreyev
Lewis Carroll
Lewis Sperry Chafer
Lilian Bell
Lloyd Osbourne
Louis Hughes
Louis Joseph Vance
Louis Tracy
Louisa May Alcott
Lucy Fitch Perkins
Lucy Maud Montgomery
Luther Benson
Lydia Miller Middleton
Lyndon Orr
M. Corvus
M. H. Adams
Margaret E. Sangster
Margret Howth
Margaret Vandercook
Margaret W. Hungerford
Margret Penrose
Maria Edgeworth
Maria Thompson Daviess
Mariano Azuela
Marion Polk Angellotti
Mark Overton
Mark Twain
Mary Austin
Mary Catherine Crowley
Mary Cole
Mary Hastings Bradley
Mary Roberts Rinehart
Mary Rowlandson
M. Wollstonecraft Shelley
Maud Lindsay
Max Beerbohm
Myra Kelly
Nathaniel Hawthrone
Nicolo Machiavelli
O. F. Walton
Oscar Wilde

Owen Johnson
P.G. Wodehouse
Paul and Mabel Thorne
Paul G. Tomlinson
Paul Severing
Percy Brebner
Percy Keese Fitzhugh
Peter B. Kyne
Plato
Quincy Allen
R. Derby Holmes
R. L. Stevenson
R. S. Ball
Rabindranath Tagore
Rahul Alvares
Ralph Bonehill
Ralph Henry Barbour
Ralph Victor
Ralph Waldo Emmerson
Rene Descartes
Ray Cummings
Rex Beach
Rex E. Beach
Richard Harding Davis
Richard Jefferies
Richard Le Gallienne
Robert Barr
Robert Frost
Robert Gordon Anderson
Robert L. Drake
Robert Lansing
Robert Lynd
Robert Michael Ballantyne
Robert W. Chambers
Rosa Nouchette Carey
Rudyard Kipling
Saint Augustine
Samuel B. Allison
Samuel Hopkins Adams
Sarah Bernhardt
Sarah C. Hallowell
Selma Lagerlof
Sherwood Anderson
Sigmund Freud
Standish O'Grady
Stanley Weyman
Stella Benson
Stella M. Francis

Stephen Crane
Stewart Edward White
Stijn Streuvels
Swami Abhedananda
Swami Parmananda
T. S. Ackland
T. S. Arthur
The Princess Der Ling
Thomas A. Janvier
Thomas A Kempis
Thomas Anderton
Thomas Bailey Aldrich
Thomas Bulfinch
Thomas De Quincey
Thomas Dixon
Thomas H. Huxley
Thomas Hardy
Thomas More
Thornton W. Burgess
U. S. Grant
Upton Sinclair
Valentine Williams
Various Authors
Vaughan Kester
Victor Appleton
Victor G. Durham
Victoria Cross
Virginia Woolf
Wadsworth Camp
Walter Camp
Walter Scott
Washington Irving
Wilbur Lawton
Wilkie Collins
Willa Cather
Willard F. Baker
William Dean Howells
William le Queux
W. Makepeace Thackeray
William W. Walter
William Shakespeare
Winston Churchill
Yei Theodora Ozaki
Yogi Ramacharaka
Young E. Allison
Zane Grey